THE PLEASURES OF LEARNING CHESS

THE
PLEASURES
OF
LEARNING
CHESS

FAIRFIELD W. HOBAN

 VAN NOSTRAND REINHOLD COMPANY
New York Cincinnati Toronto London Melbourne

First published in paperback in 1982
Copyright © 1974 by Fairfield W. Hoban
Library of Congress Catalog Card Number 81-70090
ISBN 0-442-23695-6

Printed in the United States of America
Design and layout by Vincent Priore

Van Nostrand Reinhold Company Inc.
135 West 50th Street, New York, NY 10020

Van Nostrand Reinhold Publishers
1410 Birchmount Road, Scarborough, Ontario M1P 2E7

Van Nostrand Reinhold Australia Pty. Ltd.
480 Latrobe Street
Melbourne, Victoria 3000, Australia

Van Nostrand Reinhold Company Ltd.
Molly Millars Lane,
Wokingham, Berkshire, England RG11 2PY

Originally published 1974 by Avon Books

16 15 14 13 12 11 10 9 8 7 6 5 4 3 2 1

DEDICATION

Chess has meant much to me over the years. As with music and art, it has been a way of communicating with people when there was no other common language. On one occasion, during the communal riots between the Hindus and Moslems on the Indian subcontinent, fellow chess players in a tournament saved me from bodily injury, perhaps even death, at great personal risk to themselves although I spoke little of their language and they of mine. The friendships my life has been enriched with through chess have transcended the barriers of age, sex, nationality, religion, and class.

A very large part of the motivation to write this book has involved my wish to share the pleasures of learning chess with the friends I hope to make through it, even though we will, perhaps, never meet. I therefore dedicate this book to all those who helped make it possible.

To Arnold Futterer, who taught me how to play. To my mother, Anita, who encouraged me and gave me my first set. To my wife, Jean, and my daughters, Kerrin, Susan, and Robin, who never complained about the hours and imposed silences my games and writing required. To Dr. Q. M. Hussain, K. M. Shakoor, and Cleveland Amory, many of whose ideas are incorporated in the following chapters. To Norman Cousins, who first encouraged me to write and who suggested this work. To Hal Bowser, who made innumerable suggestions of great value. To Judith Weber, whose patience and cooperation meant so much to the final result. To Linda Elliott, who devoted hours to checking the manuscript for errors.

Needless to say, if there is any merit to the end result, I do not hesitate to claim full credit for it. Mistakes and defects of omission and commission should, I think, be squarely laid at the doorsteps of all those who were so free with their comments when it was their move. Isn't that the way the game is played?

F.W.H.
Ridgefield, Connecticut
1974

CONTENTS

1.

THE WORLD OF CHESS

THE WORLD OF CHESS

FOR ALMOST FOURTEEN CENTURIES, chess has teased, tantalized, and enchanted the best minds of the world. It compresses kingdoms and their armies down to a board of sixty-four squares and thirty-two men and, through the struggles of their paladins, creates a magic that is incredible to the novitiate. But when play is started, when issue is joined, the tension and conflict on the board reveals the nature of chess as a mirror of life. Then it is easy to see that these battles are just as real to the players as Agincourt, Waterloo, and Gettysburg were to the generals who plotted the strategies and the warriors who gave their lives. Suddenly the fascination is compelling. Suddenly a parallel with the tactics of war and the intrigue of politics—a parallel with the drama of strife—is unmistakable. To first sense that Bonaparte, Metternich, Tallyrand, and Bismarck all applied basic chess stratagems in their maneuverings as empire builders is to understand this sempiternal bewitchery.

Chess was probably invented in the Indus Valley in the northern part of India in the sixth century and was first called *chaturanga*—the army game. From there it spread like quicksilver to wherever there were curious and inquiring minds. Each time it lighted, it acquired a local innovation and then moved on, richer and fuller, like a tapestry woven by countless hands. In Persia, the cry of *Sháh Mát*—checkmate—was heard, *Sháh* being the King, and *Mát* meaning fallen or defeated. Castling, the move permitting a King to flee to his fortress, was introduced in medieval Europe, initially with the King leaping alone to another, more distant square, then later leaping in conjunction with a pawn. This was a contribution of German and Italian players. The modern version of castling was adopted in France in 1620 and quickly taken up by the traditional enemies across the Channel in England. The evolution of the Bishop—from honest, ponderous war elephant to court jester and fool and then to sly and devious cleric followed the spread of chess from India to Persia, Asia Minor, the Arabies, and Europe. But when the Vikings and Crusaders whiled away the long hours on

3

their homeward-bound voyages with this new and exciting pastime, chess had already been indelibly sealed with the impress of the ancient Rajput warrior-princes. The four main sections of the Indian army—the chariots, cavalry, war elephants, and infantry—were all represented on the board with Rooks, Knights, Bishops, and pawns. The objective of the game was the traditional hunt and capture (or worse) of the enemy Rajah. Sometimes he was crushed on the field by a rampaging Rook or the consort-Queen, other times he was stabbed by the Bishop, who stealthily gained access to his tower bedroom, or surprised by a caracoling Knight.

Even the pawns were faithfully modeled after the Indian infantry. When the heavily padded foot soldier slogged into battle behind the elephants, chariots, and cavalry, he was encumbered by a massive shield that created a dead spot or hole immediately in front of him. He could strike with his spear to the forward right and to the forward left, but he was dependent on his companions-in-arms (and they often were literally just that) to protect his front. The pawn, while not up to his knees in gore as his counterpart on the battlefield was, still moves slowly, one square at a time (except on the first move, when he has the option of moving two squares—but this is a comparatively new development). He can only threaten an enemy piece or pawn to his forward right or his forward left. The square immediately in front of him is dead, a hole in which a hostile Knight, Bishop, or other piece can entrench or poise for attack. But two or more pawns, united and cooperating, are a different matter. Now they complement each other and can rout even the mightiest of opponents, as once the determined onslaughts of the spear-wielding footmen brought down war elephants and armored, mounted horsemen.

As might be expected, an intellectually challenging activity of such intensity and with so much vital force has attracted the leading minds of every era.

If Seneca thought that great genius was always touched with a little dementia, he probably had in mind some chess players.

The literature of the game abounds with tales of eccentricity, egomania, and absent-mindedness bordering on lunacy. Take, for example, Aron Nimzowitsch, one of the most erratic, volatile, and self-centered players ever to sign a tourney register. Most of the topflight masters of his day, as well as many whose games never got off the ground, have written books of reminiscences filled with "I'll-bet-you-can't-top-this" tales of his bizarre behavior. His emotional fabric, which had a warp where there should have been a woof, was ripped more than once by the strain of grueling tournaments.

Witness this tableau: the diminutive Nimzowitsch has just lost a hard-fought game to a lesser player. The room is silent as the other contestants sit in stunned disbelief. His opponent waits for a gracious comment, perhaps a "well played, old man," or even a perfunctory "congratulations." Instead, Nimzowitsch rises slowly to his feet, climbs up on his chair, and steps onto the chessboard. Then, standing among the pieces he feels have just betrayed him, he raises his hands to heaven: "God! Oh, God!" he screams. "Why did I have to lose to this idiot?"

These tactics paid off for Nimzowitsch, though, and his reputation as the Peck's bad boy of chess helped him to overwhelm his opponents, who never knew what to expect next. Not all opponents, however.

Dr. Emanuel Lasker, considered by many to have been one of the three or four top players of all time, was a past master of psychological warfare. In his chess treatises, he expounded at length on the vital importance of making every move threatening in some way.

An inveterate smoker, he always had a cigar in hand or mouth, lit or about to be lit. It is not hard, therefore, to imagine how Nimzowitsch, whose pathological aversion to smoke was well known, reacted when the redoubtable Lasker drew a cigar from his pocket at a decisive moment in their game. Nimzowitsch stared, hypnotized as Lasker slowly and carefully unwrapped it. Then he reached into his pocket, took out a box of matches, and placed it next to the board. Nimzowitsch exploded, leaping to his feet and shouting for the tournament director, Geza Maroczy, another old hand in dealing with characters of this ilk.

Maroczy strolled leisurely to the table, oblivious to Nimzowitsch's frantic efforts to hurry him up. He asked Lasker what the problem was.

Lasker looked up, feigning surprise. "Why I didn't know there was one." Then, to Nimzowitsch: "What seems to be the trouble, Aron?"

"You know very well what the trouble is," Nimzowitsch howled. "You are smoking and you know I can't stand smoke and you're doing it to put me in an unfair position and to interfere with my thinking and to ruin my game and I won't have it!"

"But I'm not smoking," Lasker replied calmly. "I'm merely holding a cigar in my hand."

"Yes, that's true," Maroczy interjected, anxious to end the brouhaha as quickly as possible.

"But that isn't the point! That isn't the point!" shrieked the now-hysterical master. "Everyone knows that Dr. Lasker has written that *the threat is much stronger than the execution!*"

It is easy to imagine who won that game.

Lasker, who had an elfin sense of humor, was World Chess Champion for more than a quarter of a century. Even in his late fifties he won a major tournament.

On the first day of one of his innumerable Atlantic crossings, he walked around the ship to meet his traveling companions and to see the vessel's facilities. In the salon he noticed a man seated at a table, pondering a chess problem. Like a needle in a compass, and with just about as much free will, Lasker was drawn toward the chessboard. The ponderer looked up.

"Do you play chess?" he asked.

"Not recently," replied Lasker truthfully.

"Well let's have a game," said his new-found friend. "Let me give you odds. I'm a strong player—I'll give you a Queen. Then, if you win, we can reduce the handicap, and we'll probably get some good games in during this voyage."

Giving a player like Lasker a Queen is like wearing ski boots and swimming against Mark Spitz or using a two-foot pole and pole-vaulting against Bob Seagren.

Lasker's fiendish humor took over. "Fine," he said, "You'll give me a Queen to start, eh?" And the omnipresent cigar materialized.

With iron control and skillful play, Lasker contrived to *lose* the first two or three games. His disappointed opponent set up the pieces again.

"Look," he said, "I don't see how I can increase these odds. I wish you'd think about your moves more carefully; I'd like to get a few good games in on this trip."

"You know what I think?" Lasker asked solemnly. "I think you get a big advantage when you take your Queen off. You see, it gives your King that empty square he can move into, just when I get my attack going. Let me take my Queen off, while you keep yours, and we'll see what happens!"

"Why that's absolutely ridiculous!" protested the unsuspecting victim. "If you can't beat me when I give you a full Queen, how can you possibly win giving me odds?"

But Lasker insisted and refused to play under any other circumstances; the risk of not having any more games for the rest of the trip overcame his adversary's objections. Lasker now proceeded to win game after game, muttering all the while, "Yah, yah, that empty square, that's a big advantage. I can always win if I have that empty square next to my King."

The baffled victim didn't find out until they docked in New York that he had been playing the strongest player in the world, a player who had a sense of humor to match his chess prowess.

Almost a half century later, another World Champion, Dr. Max Euwe, came upon his sacrificial lamb in a first-class compartment on a railway train. A fellow traveler was sitting opposite him, engrossed in a small pocket set. Noticing Euwe's interest, he asked him if he knew the moves. The World Champion admitted that he did.

"Fine, then, how about a game or two until we reach our station?" asked the man. "Although I should warn you I am a strong player, and have won the top prize in my club three times in succession."

Dr. Euwe was politely impressed, but agreed to take his chances. When they had reached their destination, the score was four to nothing in Max's favor.

"Amazing! Amazing!" observed the local hero. "That I should lose to a casual player on a train like this! *You know, back home I am known as the Euwe of my club!*"

Hand in hand with their other idiosyncrasies, Grand Masters regularly supply us with examples of absentmindedness that would send the proverbial professor to the back row of the classroom. And their tendencies in this direction receive additional impetus during tournaments and matches, when all their mental energies are concentrated on deciding which little piece of wood should be placed on which little square.

Akiba Rubinstein, contender for the World Championship, had a particularly difficult combination to solve. At adjournment time, he went down to the hotel dining room and ordered a full-course meal. He finished it somehow, signed the check, and went into the main lounge. He paused. There was something he was supposed to do now, and he couldn't remember what it was. Something he should do . . . he glanced at the clock. Of course—how could he be so forgetful? It was dinnertime. He returned to the dining room, sat down at the same table, and ordered another meal from the baffled waiter.

Strange, he thought, I don't feel at all hungry; these chess tournaments certainly kill a man's appetite.

But it's still better to have two meals than none at all. . . .

At the Carlsbad Tournament in 1929, Sir George Thomas found himself seated near Rudolf Spielmann in a local restaurant. Spielmann studied his ever-present pocket chess set, analyzing his adjourned position. The waiter served him a bowl of soup. Spielmann ignored it and continued the search for the *coup de mâitre* that would annihilate his opponent. The waiter became impatient. The entrée was ready and the soup hadn't been touched. He whispered in the master's ear, placed a spoon in his hand, and jostled his elbow. Spielmann, still con-

centrating on his portable chess set, dipped in the spoon, started it toward his mouth, and *emptied it on his lap.* He then ladled out all the soup, in the same way, while Sir George watched in stunned disbelief. Hardly an improvement over the more usual social contretemps, when the fly is in the soup!

But not all the strange experiences chess masters have in dining rooms result from their aberrations. In Mir Sultan Khan's case, it was another example of the inability of East and West to meet successfully.

Sultan Khan, one of the greatest natural players of all time, was born in India in the northwestern province of the Punjab, shortly after the turn of the century. His ability at chess came to the attention of Sir Umar Hayat Khan, a wealthy landowner, who later became A.D.C. to His Majesty King George V. Sir Umar took Sultan Khan into his household retinue as a serf, and he amused and amazed visitors when not attending to other household duties.

When Sir Umar traveled to England, he took along Sultan Khan and proudly presented him to the chess world. Khan promptly annexed the British Championship. Then came the prestigious Folkestone International Tournament of 1933. Sultan Khan amassed an impressive record against the leading Grand Masters of the world. Sir Umar was delighted. A victory celebration was called for. Sir Umar, as host, spared no expense. All the Grand Masters and local celebrities were invited. This was to be a testimonial tribute to a great new star in the chess firmament, Mir Sultan Khan.

And who waited table? Why, Mir Sultan Khan, of course. He was unable to hear all of the laudatory speeches made in his honor, for a good part of the time he carried dishes back and forth and harangued the cooks to make sure that the entrées were prepared in time.

The pure logic of the situation is unassailable: If you travel halfway around the world and bring your personal waiter and then give a dinner party—who better to wait? The dialectics of the East are awesome.

6

Not all the drama and color of chess is humorous.

In his later years, for example, Akiba Rubinstein suffered from a chronic mental disorder. This brilliant and innovative chess genius had given the world some of the most beautiful chess games ever played, but the privations he had experienced during World War I had an exacerbating effect on his game. His increasing lack of self-confidence, his memory lapses, and, finally, the weakening of his mental acumen forced his retirement from active competition. He and his mother moved to Antwerp in Belgium. Years passed. Akiba became more and more helpless, more and more dependent on his aged mother. Their income, below subsistance level, forced them to rely on charity. They lived in a one-room apartment in the poorest part of the city.

This was their situation when the Nazi juggernaut swept across the Lowland countries. All who could fled. Mrs. Rubinstein, well into her eighties, friendless, responsible for a helpless invalid, sat back to await the inevitable.

One Sunday afternoon, there was a knock at the door. The frail old woman pulled herself together and opened it. Two members of the Nazi *Schutzstaffel*, the SS, entered.

"Frau Rubinstein?"

"Yes."

"Who else is part of this household?"

"My son, Akiba."

"What does he do?"

"He's a helpless invalid. He can't even dress himself without my help. But once"—here the old woman's voice strengthened with pride—"once he was the greatest chess player in the world!"

The Nazis looked at each other. The leader spoke. "That's all irrelevant, madam.

Here are forms for you to complete. Pack your belongings and be ready to leave tomorrow morning at 8:00 A.M." They turned and stamped down the stairs.

The next morning the SS returned, but this time on a different mission.

"We're not ready yet," the old lady said frantically. "It will take us a few minutes more."

"The plans are changed, Frau Rubinstein. You and your son will not be leaving, after all. I have been given orders to issue you these identification papers, ration books, and this sum of Reichmarks. You will not be troubled any further."

The Rubinsteins survived the war and the occupation, protected by an unknown guardian, a benefactor whose name never was revealed, but whose memories of happier days and beautiful chess games had been reawakened when he saw the name of a chess immortal—Akiba Rubinstein—on his death list.

These, then, are some of the threads that have been woven into this historic tapestry. These are some of the colorful personalities and dramatic incidents that have enriched its legend, and, for some, have made it more than just a game.

Like beautiful poems that can be read and reread, the games of the great masters—Morphy, Lasker, Capablanca, Marshall, Tchigorin, Nimzowitsch, Spielmann, Alekhine, Rubinstein, Sultan Khan—and the contemporaries—Fischer, Spassky, Tal, Kotov, Botwinnick, Keres, Byrne and Euwe—can be played over and over, studied and analyzed, and made to live again.

This is the reward that lies ahead. This is the new world of adventure and splendor, grace and elegance, that every chess player may experience.

HOW
THE
PIECES
MOVE

HOW THE PIECES MOVE

SINCE THE BEST WAY to learn anything is to do it, we are going to start playing chess as quickly as possible. Get a good set, by which I mean one in which the King is between 2¾ inches and 3½ inches tall and the design a simple Staunton or standard tournament design.

Avoid the ornate and carved sets that make distinguishing the pieces more complicated than the game of chess itself. The board, which may be wood, plastic, or cloth, should also be simple without any designs other than the alternate light and dark squares which should be between 1½ inches and 2 inches on each side. The board is *always* placed so that the light square is at your right-hand corner. This is important because it determines how the pieces are placed. You and your opposing player alternate in making one move at a time. The White men move first and you are said to "have the move" when it is your turn to play. A piece is moved by transferring it from one square to another which is either vacant or occupied by an enemy piece.

Diagram 1 shows the pieces set up for a game. The White Queen is on the light-colored square and to her right is the White King. Since she is his consort and most powerful ally, this is only natural.* To the King's immediate right is his Bishop, presumably for spiritual guidance, while next come the Knight and Rook. These last three pieces are referred to as the King Bishop, the King Knight, and the King Rook. Immediately to the left of the Queen, whose morals are no better than the King's, we place the Queen Bishop, the Queen Knight, and the Queen Rook in that order. The eight

*This position of the King and Queen gives us a useful descriptive phrase—the "King side" and the "Queen side" of the chess board. See Diagram 1-A.

11

Diagram 1

Diagram 1-A

pawns are on the next rank, one in front of each piece. The Black pieces are set up in the same way, but always make sure that the Queen is on her color, that is, place the White Queen on the light square and the Black Queen on the dark square facing her. Now notice that the Black King is to the left of the Black Queen, directly opposite the White King.

In your position, seated in the command post behind your army, you and you alone are responsible for the outcome of the coming battle. You are going to make the decisions, determine the strategy, and employ the tactics that will win or lose. You are going to plan and carry out the assaults on the enemy King's stronghold, meet his armies in the field, and defend against his attacks and counterattacks. To do this, you must understand how each of your different pieces functions and how each unit can be used to greatest effect, whether in capturing hostile pieces or pawns, or in defending companions-in-arms or the position of the liege lord—the King.

All captures in chess are made as they were on the Indian battlefield; the captured soldier was removed from his position and replaced by his captor, who remained there until duty and orders called him elsewhere. When a piece captures another in chess the vanquished one is removed from the board and is out of action for the remainder of the conflict as the capturing piece occupies the square of his victim. No exceptions to this rule are permitted. However, no rule says a piece must be taken, just as on the battlefield a warrior is not obligated to slay or capture any particular opponent.

THE QUEEN

Take all the pieces off the board except the White Queen (Diagram 2). Of the forces at your disposal, she is by far the most powerful. Not the most important—that designation is reserved for the King—but without question the most powerful. In one move she can travel as far as you command

Diagram 2

12

in any direction, forward or backward, provided that she moves in a straight line and does not come up against another piece. If she comes up against one of her own pieces, then she must stop. If she comes up against a hostile piece, she can capture and position herself on the captured square or she can stop at some point before his square and watch the potential victim tremble apprehensively.

Diagram 3

The dark lines show just how the Queen can proceed as she moves out from her original square: she can stop at any empty square reachable by a straight line. The Queen in this situation is completely unobstructed by other pieces. The picture changes, though, in Diagram 3. Now that other pieces are on the scene, her range is curtailed. For example, in one move she can either capture the Knight on her immediate left or she can sail across the board and capture the Knight on her right. She can't bypass her own pawn immediately in front of her so the Black King remains shielded from her sting. The White Rook also limits the Queen's mobility, since she can only move one square in that direction. Notice how much more scope a Queen has when she is in the center of the board than when she skulks on one side. But just because she is so powerful and valuable, you must be very cautious about where you place her, so she cannot be harried by lesser pieces. Harassment of this sort can force you to waste valuable moves trying to get her safely situated.

THE ROOK

Next in value and importance to the Queen is the Rook.

(As a matter of fact, Queens and Rooks are often referred to as major pieces.) This direct descendant of the Indian war chariot has many of the characteristics of its famous ancestor—it is powerful, far-ranging, and maneuverable. Like the Queen, it can move the length or breadth of the board in one stroke, but it can't move in a diagonal direction. Again like the Queen, its range is limited only by the other pieces and pawns on the board. Set up the position in Diagram 4. The Rook on the lower left-hand corner of the board can move to any square directly in front of it or directly alongside of it. The Rook in the center of the board is limited in movement by the two pawns and the Black Queen. It can take the Black Queen or the Black pawn (note that if it takes the Black pawn, it, in turn, can be taken on the next move by the Black Queen, since she is protecting the pawn), but the White pawn is a genuine barrier. One important strength of the Rook is its ability to support the other Rook. Thus they can be deployed in tandem and penetrate deep into hostile territory with devastating effect.

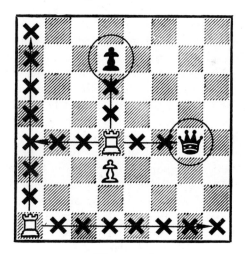

Diagram 4

If, for example, you set up your board so that the two Rooks are situated one behind the other, as in Diagram 5, you can see that

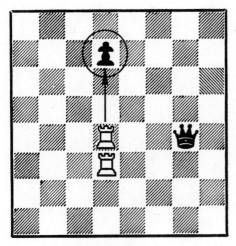

Diagram 5

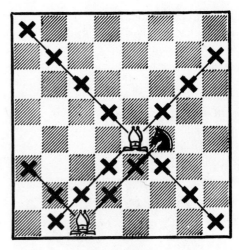

Diagram 6

the Queen's protection of the pawn is no longer worth much. If the White Rook takes the Black pawn, the Black Queen can capture the offending Rook, but then she in turn can be captured by the other Rook. Such an exchange would be a very bad bargain for the Black side, since the Queen is worth almost as much as two Rooks.

THE BISHOP

The Bishop, along with the Knight, is considered a minor piece because of the limited terrain it can cover. It can only move along the diagonals and, as a consequence, can never get off the color squares on which it begins the game. In a sense, it is rather other-dimensional to think of the two Bishops on the same side constantly moving about the chess board and never coming into contact—one permanently confined to the white squares and one to the black. Consider Diagram 6. The Bishop in the center of the board can move on any of the diagonals shown, and can stop on any of the squares along the way. Captures are made in the usual manner and this explains why the Bishop on the dark squares can, if White wishes, capture the Black Knight. But notice how much more territory is supervised by the Bishop in the center of the board. This Bishop is used with maximum efficiency.

A rather interesting point, which you've

possibly already noticed, is that between them, the Rook and the Bishop, make the same moves as the Queen. In other words, the Queen is a composite of these two pieces, but because she incorporates both their powers she is worth considerably more. Now let's add some pieces to the basic position, so that we have them set up as in Diagram 7. Here, the White Bishop on the white diagonal can take either the Black Bishop or the Black pawn. If it takes the Black pawn it can in turn be taken by the Black Queen or the Black Bishop (or, as you will shortly discover, the Black Knight). If, on the other hand, the White Bishop takes the Black Bishop first, it still threatens the Black pawn, since it is still on the same diagonal.

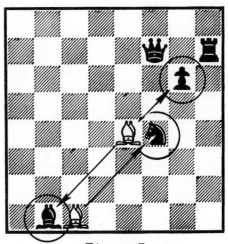

Diagram 7

14

THE KNIGHT

Now for the real fun piece—the Knight. As we mentioned earlier, this representative of the cavalry is the only piece that can leap over other pieces, both White and Black. He does this just as cavalry on the battlefield does, in what seems to be an erratic pattern, but which is, in fact, highly systematic. A Knight placed as shown in Diagram 8 can, on any one move, go to any of the squares shown, even if all the intermediate squares are occupied. Once he has reached his objective, he can capture just as the other pieces do; he takes the hapless victim off the board and occupies its square. Sometimes, as we shall see, he delivers the *coup de grâce* to the enemy King, sitting smugly complacent in what he believes to be an impregnable fortress.

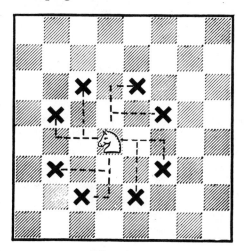

Diagram 8

Because of this unique and potent power, the opposition Knights must be watched constantly and careful consideration given to their incipient sallies and raids. The Knight in Diagram 9 can capture the Black Bishop or Knight even though pieces on his own side occupy all the intervening squares. The same applies if all the intervening squares are occupied by hostile forces.

As you can see in both diagrams, the Knight always moves to a square that is the opposite color from that on which he begins. In Diagram 8 he is on a dark square and the eight squares he can move to are all white. In Diagram 9 he is on a light square and he can move only to dark squares. *This means that, one way or another, he can cover every square on the board.* The Bishop, while more far-ranging, can only cover one half of the chess board. Something else to be observed from the position in Diagram 9 is that because the Knight is near the edge of the board the number of squares it can attack or cover is reduced to six, and a Knight on the very edge will only be a threat to four squares. This is important to remember—a Knight is most effective and keeps the most terrain under surveillance if it is centrally posted.

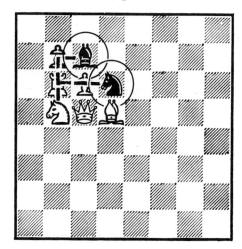

Diagram 9

THE PAWN

Don't let the size of the pawn fool you. Just as a baby adder is more poisonous than an adult viper, the spear thrust of this foot soldier can dispatch a Queen or assassinate a King. The pawn's basic move is forward, only, one square at a time. On any first move, you have the option of moving the pawn one or two squares, but after the first move of that pawn is made, the one-square-a-move limitation takes effect. Diagram 10 shows the Black and White armies arrayed for the start of a game. On your first move, you may place your pawn on square one or on square two, as you choose (and this is true for all your pawns, not just the King pawn used in this example).

Diagram 10

Diagram 11

The square immediately in front of a pawn is a dead square. That is, an enemy piece or pawn can be on it safely, while the two squares immediately ahead and adjacent to the dead square are within the pawn's range, and any foe placed on them can be captured by the pawn, which then moves to that square. This is illustrated in Diagram 11. Here the pawn can take the Knight or the other pawn, but the Bishop immediately in front is safe. As we said in Chapter I, this is analogous to the ancient Rajput foot soldier who carried a massive shield and a spear or sword into battle. The shield made the space in front of him a blind or dead area, but he could deliver a lethal blow with his spear to either side, diagonally forward. This also meant that he had to rely heavily on the Buddy System—his companions-in-arms guarded his weak spot, while he covered theirs.

As you'll learn later in more detail, pawns are strongest when they support each other as they march into enemy ambuscades and crossfires. And just as the heroic Indian foot soldier won promotion by fighting his way across the battlefield and emerging unscathed, so too our pawn wins promotion to a Knight, Bishop, Rook, or Queen if he reaches the eighth or last rank. This is called pawn promotion and is frequently decisive in the game. If, for example, all the pieces are off the board, and one side promotes his pawn to Queen, this new infusion of reinforcements, this timely arrival of the

horse troops, can change the course of the struggle. Consequently, the strategies of many games revolve around a campaign of pawn maneuverings and advances.

What good is a rule without an exception? I said previously that the pawn captured an enemy piece or pawn if the victim was on a square ahead and adjacent to the conquering midget. Now you can see that in the normal course of events, no pawn could bypass the enemy pawns; no pawn could reach the eighth rank and "Queen" without having run this pawn gauntlet, *except for the rule that permits a pawn to move two squares on its first move.* For example, if we consider the situation in Diagram 12-A where the White pawn has reached the fifth rank, the Black pawn, if it moves forward

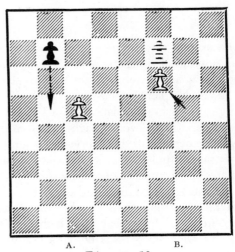

A.   B.
Diagram 12

16

one square, can be taken. But if it moves forward two squares, as it has every right to do, it would deprive the White pawn of its inalienable right to skewer it.

And so the *en-passant* rule was invented. Simply stated, this rule allows the pawn on the fifth rank to capture a pawn that attempts to leap past it in one move, just as though the victim pawn had only moved one square. The captor pawn then moves to the square on the sixth rank and in the adjacent file in the regular way as in Diagram 12-B. There is an important limitation to the rule: it must be exercised by the side having the pawn of the fifth rank immediately after the other pawn has moved, or the right to capture this way is lost. But this peculiar rule is worth knowing thoroughly. Many Kings have been humbled, many empires felled, by the clever application of an *en-passant* capture.

THE KING

The King is in a special category, because its loss means the end of the game. Hence it is not possible to equate its value with other pieces. Where it may make sense, for example, to surrender a Rook if you capture a Bishop and a Knight, or to give up a Bishop to eliminate a Rook, no such ploy involving a King is possible. But this does not mean

Diagram 13

that the King is not a powerful and valuable fighting piece. Although he has a limited range and can only move one square in any direction, once the other pieces have been retired from the fray, and he no longer has to be concerned with their vexing checks, the King can mean the difference between victory and defeat.

If you place your King as it appears in Diagram 13, he can move to any of the squares shown, providing that none of them is directly menaced by enemy artillery (notice, though, how much more effective he is in the center of the board). For example, if we add some more pieces to the board we might have the situation illustrated in Diagram 14.

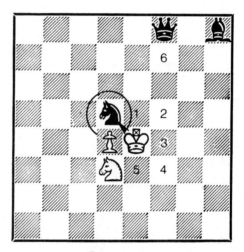

Diagram 14

Here the King cannot move into the squares occupied by the White Knight and White pawn. Squares 1,2,3,4, and 5 are barred to him because they are menaced by Black forces (square 1 by the Black Bishop, squares 2, 3, and 4 by the Black Queen and squares 3 and 5 by the Black Knight). *The King can never, under any circumstances, move into check.* However, the King can take the Black Knight since it is not protected by any other Black piece or pawn. If, for example, we move the Black Queen to square 6, she now protects her Knight (if any piece takes the Knight, it can be taken by the Queen) and the King's last escape route has been severed.

OPPOSITION

Look again at Diagram 13. Since the King can move to any square immediately adjacent to it (assuming, of course, that no hostile piece or pawn also covers that square), he can capture any unprotected hostile—even a Queen—that is impudent enough to venture that close to the royal presence. But two Kings alone on the board have an almost mystical relationship to each other. Surrounded as they are by this *cordon sanitaire*, this no-man's land, they can never draw closer than one square apart. It's as though each had a positive magnetic charge, or force field, that forever prevents cheek-to-jowl familiarity between them. It follows that if two Kings face each other, and one must move, he must move back or sideways, making way for the rival monarch. The King, then, that has this right of way is said to have the opposition. In Diagram 14-A, the White King has just moved to Q5.° Black must move, and since his pawns are blocked, he must move his King. He can move it to B2 or K2, or back to his first rank. No matter what he does, though, the White King gets free passage to attack a Black pawn (if the Black King moves to B2, the King with the opposition can move to

°These numbers (Q5, B2, and K2) refer to the square and not to the piece. This system of notation is explained in Chapter III.

Diagram 14-A

K6, etc.) and win. We will discuss the importance of having the opposition in the chapter on the end game, but, for the moment, be aware of its significance and the ultimate effect it can have on the outcome of a game.

CHECKING AND CHECKMATING THE KING

You have no moral or legal obligation to warn your opponent when you threaten one of his pieces with capture, although some players say *"en garde"* when they menace the other side's Queen. This is merely courtesy and indicates a desire not to have an otherwise good and exciting game ruined by the loss of a Queen through an oversight. After all, bringing home the trophy head of a boar, who passed out after breaking into and guzzling down your camp liquor supply while you were out in the bush, is not nearly as satisfying as tracking the beast through the jungle and subduing him in fierce man-to-ugly-monster combat.

But the case of the King is another matter entirely. Whenever he is threatened he should be warned and "check" is almost always called out as the move is made. The deploying of the enemy army comes to a halt and one of the following must take place:

1. The King in check must move to a safe square.
2. The checking piece must be captured.
3. Another piece must be thrown into the breach as a shield to protect the person of the King from the attacking piece.

If none of these moves can be made, then the King cannot be saved and is actually checkmated. The game is over.

Now to clarify some of the situations.

Here, we can illustrate all three of these escapes for the beleaguered King. White checks the King with

1. R-Q ch.   K-B4

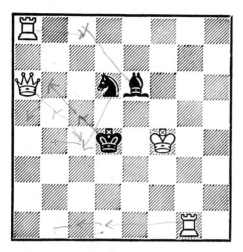

Diagram 14-B

The King has moved to a safe square, that is, a square not attacked by one of the foemen.

  2. R-B8 ch.   BxR

The checking piece has been captured and the threat to the King removed.

  3. R-B ch.   N-B5

A shielding piece, the Knight, has been put between the King and the White Rook, effectively (for the moment) saving the King.

But when none of these steps can be taken, the game is finished. Still following the same position, White might play

  4. QxN ch.   · K-N3

(The King can't take the Queen because it is supported by the Rook.)

  5. R-N ch.   K-R4

  6. Q-N5 Mate.

There is no safe square to flee to, no way to capture the Queen, and no possibility of interposing.

CASTLING

There is a special situation where the King can move more than one square. It can only occur once in a game, and the conditions surrounding this move are precise and carefully defined. Castling permits the King, in one lightning stroke, to take refuge in a prepared and fortified stronghold where he is safe, at least for the moment, from the assassin's dagger or poison ring. The value of this move is obvious—a King stranded in the center of the board risks facing the full brunt of the enemy attack. Once safely entrenched in his fortress, his forces can be used for other purposes than defending his person.

Basically, the move takes place as follows: the King moves two squares to his right (see Diagram 15-A) and the King Rook moves two squares to the left to protect his flank. This is castling on the King side. If you wish to castle on the Queen side, the King moves two squares to the left and the Queen Rook moves three squares to the right, again taking up a position protecting the King's flank (see Diagram 15-B). In both of these diagrams, the pawns are positioned as they frequently are—in front of the King's new position. *This is not a requirement, but it emphasizes the defensibility usually found in the King's new position.*

King-Side Castling
Diagram 15-A

Notice that this is the only time in a game that two pieces are moved at one time. There are stringent requirements that must be met before the King can castle.

1. Neither the King nor the Rook he is castling with can have moved.

2. The King may not be in check at the time of castling.

3. The King may not pass over or land on a square under the attack of an enemy piece.

4. All of the squares between the King and the Rook he is castling with must be vacant (i.e., there may be no pieces of either color on these squares).

reasons; the King Rook has moved and the Black Queen Bishop threatens a square over which the White King would be forced to pass. The White King can castle Queen side (we assume that the White Queen Rook has not moved). The Black King may not castle on his King side because of White's Queen Bishop, but the Black King can castle on the Queen side even though White's King Bishop is attacking the Black Rook and even though the White Queen covers a square (Knight 8) over which the Black Rook will be forced to pass.

Queen-Side Castling
Diagram 15-B

Diagram 16

After you have these limitations firmly in mind, consider how they affect the castling possibilities in Diagram 16. For example, and assuming that neither King has moved, can White castle? Can Black?

First, we will consider the White King's chances for escaping the dangers of the exposed center of the board. Castling on the King side cannot be accomplished for two

In the next chapter we will introduce you to the art of reading the mysterious notations you have probably seen in newspapers and magazines which are used to record chess games and problems. Once you have taken the simple step of learning to read the language of chess, your life will never be the same again, for you will become an active adventurer, Florentine intriguer, and calculating chief of staff all at the same time.

3.

THE SYSTEM OF CHESS NOTATION

THE SYSTEM OF CHESS NOTATION

IT DOES NOT SEEM POSSIBLE that a simple and satisfactory method could be invented that would accurately record all the moves 32 pieces can make on 64 squares in a game that can last for 100 moves or more. And yet that is just what the system of chess notation most commonly employed in the Western world does. The average number of legal moves available to a player on his turn is about 30. If he looks forward 5 moves (which is pretty good!), we are talking about 30^5, or 24,300,000 possibilities, and yet, if anyone wanted to, every one of these moves could be accurately recorded.

Here is how the system works. Each square has a name and each piece has a name, but once you learn how to set the pieces up, you have all the information you need to read chess notations.

The horizontal rows are called *ranks* and the vertical rows are called *files* (Diagrams 17 and 17-A). The ranks are numbered one through eight, beginning with the rank nearest the player, while the files are named after the piece that is set on the first rank at the beginning of the game. For simplicity's sake we abbreviate the names of the pieces by using their first letters. Thus the Queen becomes *Q* and the King becomes *K*. To avoid confusion between the King and the Knight, the Knight is called either *Kt* (the old-fashioned way) or *N*, which is the abbreviation used in this book. The following chart shows the abbreviations and the symbols used and recaps some of the information given in Chapter I.

Piece	Abbreviation	Symbol White: Black:
King	K	
King's Bishop	KB	
King's Knight	KN	
King's Rook	KR	
Queen	Q	
Queen's Bishop	QB	
Queen's Knight	QN	
Queen's Rook	QR	
Pawn	P	

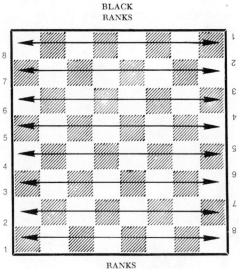

Diagram 17

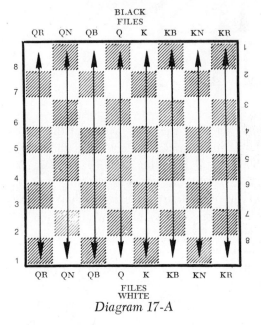

Diagram 17-A

the first square in each file the square after the piece, as QB and KN, meaning the QB1 or KN1. Notice that the same system is used for the Black side, so that the White QR2 is QR7 for Black and the White QN7 is Black's QN2. In other words, although the files are the same for Black and White, the ranks are not, and White's eighth rank is Black's first, as Diagram 17 shows. Confusion as to which square we mean when we say a piece moves to, say, KB3 is avoided because we know which side, Black or White, is moving. If it is White's move, the piece goes to White's KB3 and if it is Black's move, the piece goes to Black's KB3.

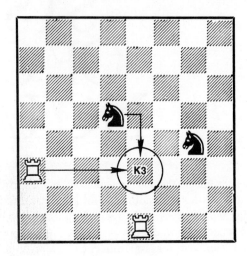

Diagram 18

(The pawn is named after the piece it is placed in front of at the beginning of the game—the *QP*, the *KP*, etc.)

Now take a look at Diagram 17-A. Each file, as we said, gets its name from the piece originally placed on it when the game is set up. Starting at the far left, the first file is the Queen's Rook file, or, as abbreviated, the *QR* file. Next to it is the *QN* file, then the *QB, Q, K, KB, KN,* and *KR* files. The squares are called by their numbers—*QR2, KB3, QN7,* and so on, while for simplicity's sake we omit the number 1, and just call

Using a dash (-) to show that a piece moves, we can say R-Q3, meaning that the Rook moved to the third square on the Queen's file. Using an x to show that a piece has captured another piece, we can say RxN, meaning that the Rook has captured the Knight, and is now occupying its square.

Sometimes, to avoid ambiguities, we have to specify which Rook went to K3 or which Knight moved to capture that Rook on the next move. In Diagram 18, White can move either Rook to K3, so the simple R-K3 leaves us guessing. There are several ways of being more specific; we can write R(QR3)-K3 or R(3)-K3 or, if we remember from the beginning of the game which Rook was the original QR and which was the original KR, we can say QR to K3 (some of the grander antique sets have a tiny Q or K marked on the Rooks and Knights so that these pieces can be identified throughout the game). The Bishops, since they are trapped on the color they start out on for the entire game, never lose their identity; the White KB is always on the white diagonal and the White QB is always on the black diagonal. Still referring to Diagram 18, after R(3)-K3, N(4)xR, which Knight was it that acted so vigorously? Reflection shows that only one Knight qualifies—the one on Black's Q4, since the other Knight is on Black's KN5, and when we move the Black pieces, we always use the Black designation for the squares.

Sometimes it is necessary to show which Bishop moves, as in this example:

Diagram 19

Here, if we say BxN, either Bishop can make the called-for move, so we have to be more precise, with B(3)xN, or, as is more often done, KBxN. If the Black King is on the Black Queen square, as shown in Diagram 20, we can note the move as BxN without pinpointing which Bishop does the taking, *because the position itself prevents ambiguity.* Here, if QBxN (that is, if the Bishop on KB4xN), then the move would read BxN ch. and this means that only one Bishop can take one Knight without putting the opponent's King in check. The abbreviation ch., standing for check, clearly discriminates between the two possible Bishop

moves and shows which one was played.

Diagram 20

This brings us to a few other abbreviations that indicate special moves. When the King castles on the King's side, we use the notation 0-0, and when castling takes place on the Queen's side, we use 0-0-0. If a piece in moving *exposes* the opponent's King to a check, this is called a discovered check, and is indicated by the abbreviation dis. ch. (Diagram 21). If the "unmasking" piece also checks the opponent's King, and he is subjected to a double check, this is abbreviated as dbl. ch. (Diagram 22). Here the White Queen just moved to N3, checking the Black King. Black moves his Rook to B5, shielding his king and subjecting the White King to a double check—one from the Rook and one from the Bishop.

Whenever you see a move preceded by three or more dots like this—1. ... P-K4— you are being told that it is Black's move and that White has made the previous move. In other words, the dots really represent a space to put the White move in, but for some reason (perhaps it was given on the page before or, if there is a diagram, before the diagram) it isn't necessary to give it or repeat it at that point. Of course, if some indication of which side just moved isn't made, you can't tell which pawn moved to which King's fourth square. And this brings us to an important point in notation: always make sure, when you are writ-

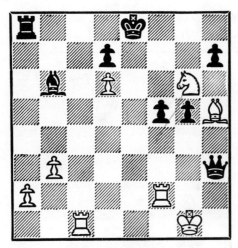

1. N-B4 dis. ch.

Diagram 21

1. Q-N3 ch.   R-B5 dbl. ch.

Diagram 22

ing games, that the move you record is clear and unequivocal. Is there any question as to which side is moving? Is there any other like piece that could make the same or a similar move? Is there any ambiguity as to which piece or pawn has been captured or has done the taking? If so, add a descriptive letter or number to clear up the possible confusion. If a pawn takes another, show that as KPxP and if the KP can take one of two pawns, show that the KPxQP or whatever is necessary to make the picture crystal clear. When the notation reads PxP (e.p.) it means pawn takes pawn *en passant*.

Frequently, when you see games recorded in newspapers or chess publications, a move has an exclamation point or question mark immediately following it. This means just what it says:

> ! = Good move
> !! = Extraordinary move
> ? = Poor move or mistake

You will also see press references to points won or lost in tournament play. The prevailing custom is to give the winner of a tournament game one point, the loser no points, and each player one half of a point if the game is drawn. This will be shown as

> F. Marshall—1,   A. Alekhine—0
> or
> F. Marshall—½,   A. Alekhine—½

Don't be concerned if all of this seems like too much to remember. You are past the worst of it and now we'll go through a famous classical game with each of the moves carefully explained, so that you can begin to sample the thrills and excitement that have fascinated men and women since the dawn of history.

DE LEGAL VERSUS SAINT BRIE

The scene: Paris. The year: 1750. The White pieces are under the command of DeLegal, strongest player of his day until his famous student, the great André Philidor, surpassed him. Black is played by Chevalier Saint Brie, presumably a lover of exceptional cheeses.

DeLegal opened with:

1. P-K4

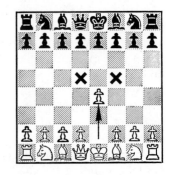

Diagram 23

Since White has the first move, White can launch his attack first. This pawn strikes at the vital center of the board and threatens the two squares marked by X.

Diagram 24

1 . . . P-K4

Black replied with the same move and signified his intention to meet the attack head-on and to contest every attempt by White to invade Black territory. This move doesn't dispute the control over the two squares White obtained with his first move, but exercises a similar threat over two important squares in the White sphere of influence—very much the way feinting armies seize undefended border towns when hostilities break out between warring nations.

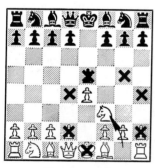

Diagram 25

2. N-KB3

White's Knight has moved onto the battlefield and threatens the unprotected Black pawn. From this commanding position, it also makes its presence felt on all the other seven squares within its range. The most important of these from Black's point of

view are (Black's) Q5, N4, and R5, because now Black cannot place a piece on these squares without risking its capture. For example, if Black now played 2. ... Q-N4 or 2. ... Q-R5, White could play 3.NxQ, and the Black forces would be deprived of their most important fighting piece. But the immediate problem Black has is the defense of the Black pawn on K4, and so Saint Brie plays:

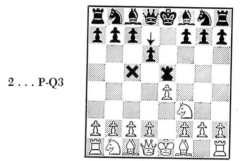

2 . . . P-Q3

Diagram 26

Now the pawn on K4 is supported by his fellow warrior. If the White Knight takes him, the Knight will, in turn, be captured by this back-up pawn and, because a Knight is worth far more than a pawn, only the most compelling reasons could justifiy such a sacrifice.

3. B-B4

Diagram 27

This move is even more threatening to Black than the previous Knight play; the Bishop's effective range extends all the way into the Black stronghold to Black's KB2.

Thus, the King's august person itself is menaced.

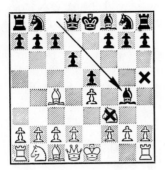

Diagram 28

3 . . . B-N5

Black responds with a counter-thrust. This Bishop move pins the White Knight to his Queen. Now if the Knight shielding the Queen moves, the Queen can be captured by the Bishop.

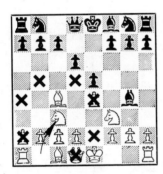

Diagram 29

4. N-B3

With the entrance of this Knight on the field of battle, White has almost all of his light units (consider the Queen and the Rooks as the heavier or more important part of the army) involved in the attack.

Black is caught in a dilemma; only one of the Black pieces has been developed, that is, put into active status where it can exert pressure on the opposing forces or counteract some of their threats. The other Bishop is severely restricted by the pawn on Q3. To get it into the fray, Black plays:

4 . . . P-KN3

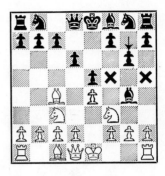

Diagram 30

The aim is to put the Bishop on N2 as soon as possible. But White's army is poised for the attack and White strikes with:

5. NxP!

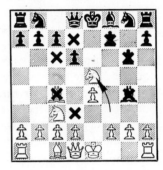

Diagram 31

And a beautiful combination is born. This Knight, although a shield for the White Queen, now has a more important role to play. From this new vantage point, White threatens the pawn on B7 (remember the White B7 is the same as the Black B2) for a second time (it was already under attack by the White Bishop) and now also can capture the Bishop on N5 if it doesn't move. But what can Black do? If he moves the Bishop to a safe square such as K3, White has won a pawn and a very valuable one at that—the KP. This is too humiliating to accept, and, besides, did White make a serious error in leaving his Queen *en prise*? This impudence must be punished and so Black plays:

28

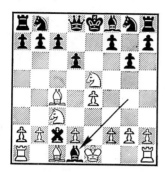

Diagram 32

5 ... BxQ?

The bait has been taken and the trap springs shut!

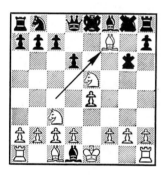

Diagram 33

6. BxP ch.

The White Bishop is protected by the Knight, so the King is legally barred from taking it, since he then could be captured. No other Black piece is in a position to be of any help to the King in his hour of need, and there is nought for it but to pick up the royal robes and make a dignified escape (the King cannot remain where he is because the Bishop threatens to do him in on the next move). But to what square? Q2 is under attack by the White Knight, the squares of either side are occupied by the Queen and Bishop, both of whom stand goggle-eyed at this affront to their liege lord, and this leaves only the haven of K2.

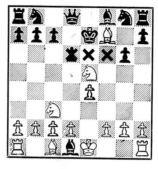

Diagram 34

6 ... K-K2

But now comes the mortal blow.

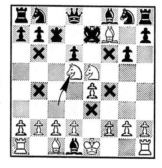

Diagram 35

7. N-Q5 MATE

The King cannot return to his original square or K3 because the Bishop covers them. He cannot remain where he is because the Knight on Q5 will capture him, and this same Knight also prevents his escape via his B3. Q2 is, of course, still attacked by the White Knight on K5, and all the other squares are glutted with his completely disorganized troops.

How early in the game did DeLegal see this combination? Probably sometime shortly after Black's third or fourth move, when he first noticed that the Black forces were not being deployed quickly enough for an adequate defense of their King. Then he saw his opportunity and struck. But remember that DeLegal was the leading player of his day, and had an intuitive feel for the potentialities of positions of this sort that was sharpened by countless hours of competitive play. After you have mastered the essentials of the game and tested basic strategy in the crucible of battle, you will be well on your way to creating exciting and rewarding combinations of your own.

Another notation system, which complements the one discussed in this chapter, is the Forsyth.° This is not used in transcribing games, but rather is an extremely easy and accurate way of recording positions. It can be very helpful when adjourning a tournament game or studying a combination. Starting at the far side of the board, the empty squares are indicated by numbers. The ordinary initial letters are used to represent the pieces, lower case for the Black pieces and upper case for the White. To demonstrate, let us record the following diagram:

DUS-CHOTIMIRSKY

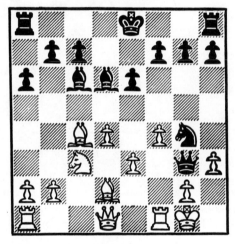

MARSHALL

Diagram 35-A

Starting with the eighth rank, we show a Black Rook on the first square, three empty squares, the Black King, two empty squares, and the Black Rook. Thus:

r 3 k 2 r
1 p p 2 p p p
p 1 b b p 3
8
2 B P 1 P n 1
2 N 1 P 1 q P
P P 1 B 2 P 1
R 2 Q 1 R K 1

Notice that each line must total eight for the eight squares and that each square must be accounted for either as part of a number or as an upper-case letter or a lower-case letter (for the White and Black pieces).

This position, by the way, is a fascinating one. Frank Marshall, many times the United States Champion and one of the first world Grand Masters, played White against a strong Russian master, Dus-Chotimirsky. Black had just moved his Queen from KR5 to N6, threatening to checkmate White in two ways, either with QxNP mate (since the Queen is protected by the Bishop, it cannot be taken by the King) or with Q-R7 mate (here the Queen is protected by the Knight, which also blocks an escape route for the White King at B2). Dus-Chotimirsky leaped up excitedly, ran to the next room, and shouted in heavily accented English, "Poor Marshall is dead!" The other players in the tournament hurried back with him and clustered around the board in time to see Marshall calmly meet both threats by playing QxN! Dus-Chotimirsky groaned, "Oh, oh, Marshall not dead, I dead!"

°Invented by David Forsyth of Scotland at the turn of the century.

4.

SOME SPECIAL RULES AND GUIDELINES

SOME SPECIAL RULES AND GUIDELINES

THERE, YOU HAVE DONE IT! You have actually played through an entire chess game—seen how the pieces move, how the overall battle plan is executed, and how the two armies attack and parry, threaten and deploy, until one of the Kings, his defenses breached, is lost. In fact, you are almost ready to replay the games you read about in newspapers and in chess columns in magazines. Almost, but not quite: there are a few special rules and precepts with which you must be familiar in order for some situations on the chessboard to make sense to you.

For example, in game after game why do we find a certain pattern emerging in the exchange of pieces? Bishops and Knights are exchanged freely for other Bishops and Knights. A Rook may be exchanged for a Bishop or Knight and two or more pawns, but rarely is a Queen exchanged voluntarily for less than two Rooks or three minor pieces (the Knights and Bishops). Sometimes a Queen will be exchanged for a Rook and a Bishop or Knight and one or more pawns. All of these relative values have been developed over the years in master play and over-the-board practice, and they represent the best available opinion on how to proceed when the possibility of an exchange of men materializes out of the smoke and dust of battle. Should you avoid an exchange or press for it? Consider the following chart of relative values, which is a sort of all-other-things-being-equal chart. Because it is based on opinion, and opinion only, it may be suspended whenever you choose. Using the pawn as the unit of measurement, the pieces (except the King, which, as we said before, is invaluable) are given a market value.

$$
\begin{aligned}
\text{Queen} &= 9 \text{ pawns} \\
\text{Rook} &= 5 \text{ pawns} \\
\text{Bishop} &= 3 + \text{ pawns} \\
\text{Knight} &= 3 \text{ pawns}
\end{aligned}
$$

This means that, on the average, if you can capture two Rooks for your Queen, you have slightly the better of it, while if you lose your Rook in capturing a Bishop or Knight (called "losing the exchange"), you have gotten the short end of the stick. You come out ahead of your opponent if you manage to get four pawns for your Bishop or three pawns for your Knight. But all of these are rules of thumb and in a particular situation you may emerge victorious if you get only a Knight for your Queen if you also, in the process, push home a mating attack. Therefore, judge each situation on its own merits and then determine your best course of action.

Set up the position in the following diagram.

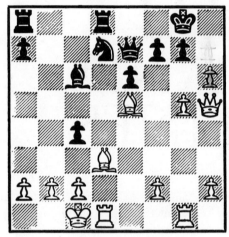

SPIELMANN
Magdeburg, July 1927
Diagram 36

White played

1. QxRP!

This threatens mate in two ways—either QxNP mate or Q-R7 ch., K-B; Q-R8 mate, and so Black plays

1. . . .   PxQ

Now, based exclusively on our table of values, it looks as though White has been shortchanged by about eight pawns worth, but

2. PxP dis. ch.   K-B
(from the Rook way back on the Knight square!)
3. R-N8 ch.!   KxR
(forced)
4. P-R7 ch.   K-B
5. P-N8 (Queen) mate.
   P-R8

This example was chosen because it is a clear illustration of the fact that material is just one of the factors affecting the outcome; the peculiarities of the position must also be taken into account. Here White gave up a Queen and a Rook for only two pawns—*and the game.*

CHECKMATES

This brings us to what checkmate, the battle cry of the victor, really is. As we have seen, it is illegal for the King to move onto a square where he is threatened by a unit of the opposing army, including the opposing King. This makes sense because the loss of the King spells the end of the game, and chess is too logical to permit a finale such as a King raising his head above the parapet and being winged by a stray arrow. But what if the King is menaced where he stands, cannot move to another square, the piece threatening him cannot be captured, and no loyal subject is near enough to throw in his body as a shield? Then we have checkmate—meaning, in effect, that there is nothing that can be done to save the august being. A primitive but clear example is presented in Diagram 37-A.

A.   B.
Diagram 37

The Black King, his back against the wall, cannot move into the Knight file because of the position of the White King. He cannot stay where he is because the Queen threatens to take him on the next move. He has no pieces to place between himself and the hostile Queen, and the Queen cannot be captured. Hence he is mated.

In Diagram 37-B, with White to move, there are several tantalizing possibilities. If White plays

| 1. Q-R3 ch. | B-R4 |

then the instant mate is thwarted by the shielding action of the Black Bishop. But what if White plays

| 1. Q-N7 ch. | K-R4 (forced) |

2. Q-N5 mate
    or
2. Q-R7 mate

Back to Diagram 37-A for a moment. We would have the same result if we substituted a Rook for the Queen because this is the standard mating position in a King-and-Rook-versus-a-King ending. We will discuss the basic mates, that is, how to mate with different pieces, in the chapter on the end game.

STALEMATES

If a position develops in which the player cannot make a legal move *and the King is not in check*, the King is said to be stalemated. He is pinned to his square as shot and shell whip by him from all directions, but without hitting him, and none of his other pieces can move. Some of the trickiest footwork is seen when a losing side develops a draw as a way out of an otherwise hopelessly lost position. First, to grasp the essentials of a stalemate position, consider the following examples.

In Diagram 38, the Black King is stalemated. None of the pawns can advance, the Black Rook is pinned to the King (by the Bishop on QR3) and cannot move legally, and the King is hemmed in by the Bishop, Queen, and pawn. If it were White's move, there would be five separate mates in the offing (R-R8, Q-N8, BxR, Q-R8 and Q-N7), but it is Black's move and the game is a draw, a moral victory if ever there was one.

Black to move
Diagram 38

Or consider the following:

Diagram 39

Black's forces have been so depleted, one wonders if his command post has been electronically bugged. White has four separate mates on the move (Q-N5, Q-N6, R-R7, and R-N6). Unfortunately for White, however, it is Black's move and he has a legal move, not with the King or pawns—they are completely hemmed in. Not so the Rook. Free as a bird, it can make all sorts of moves, and then White can deliver the *coup de grâce*. Unless—

| 1. . . . | R-B7 ch.!! |

Now, what can White do? If he takes the Rook with his King, Black has no legal moves left and the stalemate splits the point. He moves his King away with

2. K-Q3

No good. The Black Rook clings to him like a thief to a pardon:

2. . . .   R-B6 ch.!

And whenever the White King flees this albatross, this reminder of his past sins (that is, greed and lost opportunities) hangs around his neck. Black has salvaged his game and pulled off a draw.

How do you avoid this sort of chess embarrassment? First, always be wary of any position where your opponent's moves are limited—where his pawns are blocked and he only has one or two free pieces to move, and where his King is stuck on a square surrounded by booby traps and land mines so that he *cannot* move.

When you move in for a mate, try to force your opponent's King with checks, since this is the real antidote to the poison of stalemate. In Diagram 40 the White King and Queen are positioned for a mate. If White moves his Queen to Q6 (presumably planning a mate with Q-B7 on the next move), the Black King is stalemated. But if White plays Q-Q7ch., K-N (forced) and Q-N7 mate.

Diagram 40

And, if you are in a losing situation, remember that your archers may still have one last lethal shaft in their quivers, the one that can equalize and force a stalemate. Plan your moves carefully. Put your King in his solitary cell. Use up your pawn moves as stealthily as possible. Sacrifice a free piece here and there until you are ready to spring the trap and surprise your foe.

In this predicament:

Diagram 40-A

White, if he has the move, mates easily with Q-B7 or Q-B8. But what if Black has the move? A careful study of Black's resources shows that somehow White has missed opportunities and may be susceptible to the same trap he has planned for the Black King. Black first tries to visualize a favorable position (in this instance, either a stalemate or one in which he can exchange his Rook for the White Queen, ending the game in a draw in both cases). Then he tries to work out the move or moves that will give him the result he seeks.

1. . . .   R-N3 ch!

This gives White a Horson's choice, for if

2. KxR,

Black has no legal move he can make. Stalemate. If White moves his King away, with

2. K-B5   RxQ
3. KxR draw

36

DRAWS

There is another kind of game that also ends in a draw—the negotiated treaty between two *equal* military forces that seek to avoid useless carnage (and who are both afraid, usually, that a loss is distinctly possible). Each side carefully evaluates its prospects for winning and comes to the conclusion that they are minimal. A draw can then be agreed upon. If strict tournament rules are being followed, however, remember the Black pieces must have made at least thirty moves.

1936 Nottingham International Tournament
TYLOR

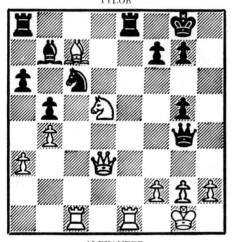

ALEXANDER

Diagram 41

An analysis of the position does not show either side with a marked advantage. Black has an incipient mating threat at N7 (since his Bishop and Queen are aimed at that square) and has another threat or two, but White can parry these easily.

| 1. Q-KN3 | QxQ |

So much for the mating possibilities.

2. RPxQ	N-K4
3. RxN	RxR
4. BxR	BxN

Drawn.

Then there is the situation in which one side or the other forces a draw by catching his opponent's King in a perpetual check. This is just what it sounds like, for the checking side, usually inferior in strength or position, does not have sufficient forces on hand for checkmating the harried King, but can, however, check endlessly. Since this cannot be resolved, a draw is declared.

1936 Nottingham International Tournament
TYLOR

WINTER

Diagram 42

White does not have much in the way of prospects and seeks to save his game by forcing a perpetual check. His first move in this strategic ploy is aimed at leveling some of the defenses surrounding the enemy King's fortress with his heavy artillery.

1. R-B3	N-K4
2. R-N3	P-KN4
3. P-R4	P-R3
4. PxP	RPxP
5. RxP ch.!	PxR
6. QxP ch.	K-B2
7. Q-R5 ch.	K-N2

Drawn. The Black King cannot escape the checks of the White Queen.

There are two other conditions under which a draw may be imposed by the rules: (1) if the same position repeats itself three separate times in one game with the same player having the move; and (2) when one of the players demands that his opponent mate him within fifty moves. *But in this instance, the count starts over again each time a piece is exchanged or a pawn moved.*

37

TOUCH MOVE RULE

The FIDE* rules, of course, only apply in matches, tournaments, and when players mutually agree. The rules provide that a touched piece must be moved (or captured, if the touched piece is the opponent's) unless the player advises his opponent *beforehand* that he is adjusting or *j'adoubing* (a French phrase that has come into common chess usage). But let me suggest that you get into the habit of moving a piece if you have touched it and of never taking a move back after you have completed it. There are very few battlefields where a major may shout to the commanding officer of an enemy ambushing squad that he would like to call the whole thing off and pull his men back from the pass—where he got them trapped through an oversight.

Once you acquire the habit of following the international rules, you will not run the risk of forfeiting games by overlooking this technicality. In addition, your whole play will be sharpened as you consider all the possibilities, thus anticipating traps and pitfalls before they occur. This makes for skillful play and lays the groundwork for an eventual master performance.

* *Fédération Internationale Des Échecs—the gov-*erning world chess organization.

5.

CHESS-
90%
TACTICS,
10%
STRATEGY

CHESS- 90% TACTICS, 10% STRATEGY

ALTHOUGH THE DISTINCTION between strategy and tactics in chess is baffling to new players, the basic concept is simple and easy to grasp. Strategy involves the overall planning for the attack, the master plan for winning the game. Tactics are more limited in scope, may be freshly formulated from move to move, and constantly revised to meet the exigencies of the moment. Out on the battlefield, a platoon leader may be ordered to capture a hill against terrible odds. Four hours later the same hill may be surrendered without a fight. This tactical exercise is part of the strategic plans that have been devised by the general staff and it hopefully has some ultimate significance. Tactical and strategic plays have many common characteristics. However, tactical plays are more limited, and their significance less.

Richard Teichmann, known as the "Richard the Third" of chess, because he finished in third place in many international tournaments, once observed that "chess is ninety-nine percent tactics." He then proceeded to give us some of the best examples of strate-

gic planning in chess literature. The interdependence of the two is clear. After all, if through a tactical maneuver you can win a Queen or Rook from your opponent, you may modify your strategic plan to take full advantage of your new superiority of forces.

But before we go into the different tactical weapons you will use in the opening, middle, and end game, let us consider some of the factors that influence the planning of a grand strategy.

Chess, like the martial struggles it portrays so faithfully, is an amalgam of three essential components: time, space, and material. If general-staff strategy in a military contest between warring nations results in control over a greater portion of the contested terrain or in heavier reserves being committed to battle, or in more mobility in the shifting of its armies to different theaters of war, that particular side will probably prevail.

The parallel is clear. Control over a larger portion of the chessboard is a clear advantage, as is material superiority. Both are easily discerned. Not so with an advantage in

41

time, which is harder to achieve or appreciate. Each player has the same number of moves, but one may waste his while the other strikes with telling effect. For example, you can advance your KP-K4 in one move or two. If you use two, you have lost a tempo, and some cognoscenti hold that three tempi are equal to one pawn. The judicious use of your moves—the saving of tempi—can be translated into material gain or space advantage in the middle game when your superior development and well-positioned men launch their attack.

The subtleties of chess magnify when each player has a marked advantage in different elements. Then a gladiator contest may seesaw across the board with the outcome undecided until the very end.

The first problem you face at the chessboard when you're ready to make your opening move is, of course, which piece to move and where. Since only the Knight can leap over other pieces, you have twelve possible moves—eight pawn moves and two moves (R3 or B3) by each of the Knights. What part of the unoccupied area in front of your assembled troops do you want to move into? The four squares in the immediate center of the board are the most important strategically. The side that controls them, *either by occupation or by indirect influence from a distance,* has a stranglehold on the opposing forces. From this heartland, attacks can be launched, campaigns in the

wings can be supported, and counterattacks thwarted. The side controlling these squares, and, to a lesser extent, the twelve squares adjacent to them shown in the diagram has greater mobility—that is, can shift his army and attack from one theater of conflict to another in a shorter time and with fewer moves—than the other.

His pieces, well posted in the center, have greater scope and exert their influence or more terrain than comparable units located less effectively.

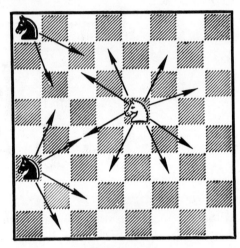

Diagram 44

Consider the location of these three Knights. The White Knight in the center of the board strikes at eight vital squares, the Knight in the corner only at two, and the Knight on the edge of the board covers four

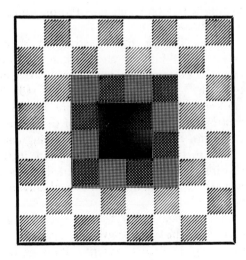

Diagram 43

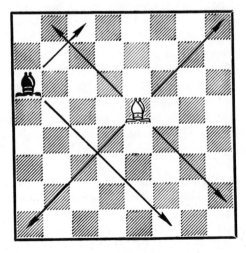

Diagram 45

42

squares, or only one half as many as does the well-placed horse.

The White Bishop on K5 can take aim at a maximum of thirteen squares, while a poorly placed Bishop such as the one on R3 is limited to only seven squares, and is just about one half as effective. Similarly with the Queen. Centrally placed she is much more dominating and imposing, exerting her influence over twenty-seven squares instead of twenty-one when she is relegated to the corner of the board.

All of these considerations suggest that pawn moves or Knight moves aimed at establishing a forward and centralized outpost as soon as possible are part of an effective strategic plan. And, in fact, most openings do begin with P-K4 or P-Q4 or KN or QN-B3. Most, but not all. Some openings defer the attempt to obtain control of the center until after the other side has revealed its plans and has progressed too far in its strategy to withdraw or even modify easily.

Before we go further into how openings, middle games, and end games are best conducted, we are going to explore some of the many different tactical weapons that you should include in your armory. Then, as you develop and deploy your troops for maximum effectiveness in battle, you will be able to employ these tactical weapons as opportunities arise. At the same time you must be on constant guard to prevent tactical disasters from confounding your general staff and routing your forces.

THE PIN

A piece is considered pinned when it cannot move away from its square because of the dire consequences that would occur, or because it is legally barred by the rules of the game from moving. Let us consider the position in Diagram 46-A.

Black has just moved his Bishop to N4 to attack the White Rook and, in doing this, has fallen into a trap. White plays

    1. R-N3, pinning the Bishop to
        the King.

Now Black is prevented from moving his Bishop, since to do so would expose the Black King to attack by the Rook—an illegal

A.   B.

Diagram 46

move. Furthermore, the Rook threatens to capture the Bishop on the next move and the Black King is too far away to support his piece. Black does have what seems to be a saving move, however, with

    1. ...   P-R3

Now if the Rook takes the Bishop, the pawn can take the Rook, and White has lost the Exchange. But White has another tactical ploy at hand.

    2. P-R4

Thus White threatens to take the Bishop with the pawn and exchange the other pawn as well. Black is without further parries.

In Diagram 46-B, the tables are somewhat turned. Black plays

    1. ...   N-B4

Attacking the White Rook, and White, leaping first and looking after, plays

    2. R-B4

True, this does pin the Knight to the King, and isn't that what we're talking about? But don't pin just for the sake of pinning. Look to the consequences first and make sure you are the trapper and do not become the trapped. Black plays

    2. ...   2. B-K4!

pinning the Rook to the White King. White has a little assist, though, in his KP (notice that the White King cannot even go to his Rook's assistance because the Knight bars him from the one square, N3, from which he could support his Rook). He can place the KP on K3 and support the Rook (not on K4 attacking the Knight, because the Bishop takes the Rook with a check, the King must move, and then the Knight, no longer pinned, can move away), but this is small solace.

There are other pins, almost as dangerous, where the pinned piece can be legally moved, but the anguish is just as real.

A.   B.

Diagram 47

Black moves (Diagram 47-A)

1. . . .   B-B6

attacking the Rook and the pawn. But White counters with

2. R-QB

pinning the Bishop. But pinning it to what? you ask. Look at the position. If the Bishop stays, it is taken by the Rook and if it moves, say with

2. . . .   BxP

then White has

3. R-B8 mate!!

It is an effective pin, after all, even though

the Bishop was not legally barred from moving.

Now consider this same position with one slight change: place the White King on R4 instead of on R2:

1. . . .	B-B6
2. R-B	P-N4 ch.!
3. KxP	BxP

The Bishop is saved. The mate threat by the Rook has disappeared because the Black King has an escape hatch at N2, the square vacated by the pawn.

In Diagram 47-B, the pin is somewhat different. Here Black plays

1. . . .   R-R

pinning the Knight to the White Rook. If the Knight moves away, the Rook falls. For the moment, the Knight is safe, but White can see that in an instant the Black Bishop will join in the sport of Knight-baiting by moving to B3, where there will be two pieces attacking the Knight and only one, the Rook, defending it—a sure formula for losing a piece. However, White has some remedies at hand. He can play either

2. R-R2

and then when the Bishop attacks the Knight with

2. . . .	B-B3
3. N-B3	

protecting his Rook with the Knight, or White can play

2. K-B2

This is another way of saving because now when Black attacks with the Bishop, White can play 3.R-K ch., removing the Rook from harm's way and giving him time to slip away the Knight.

Sometimes the pin can be broken by driving off the pinning piece with a barrage of pawn attacks as in Diagram 48, taken from the Sicilian Defense. The White Bishop has pinned the Knight to the King and is frustrating Black's development plan. White threatens to advance his Queen pawn and thus build up a strong center. Black takes the first step to eliminate the pin with:

Diagram 48

Diagram 49

| 1. . . . | P-QR3 |
| 2. B-R4 | P-QN4 |

And that's the end of that pin! Black could also have played 1. . . . B-Q2, freeing the Knight from its role as a shield for the King.

Pins can be as vicious as black-widow spiders, but they are not impossible to cope with, as we have seen. If you get caught in their entangling web, don't panic. Search for a possible escape with a check or other saving move or sequence of moves.

DOUBLE ATTACKS

These antipersonnel weapons are in the arsenal of every top-notch chess player and can frequently save the day when all seems lost. The essential ingredient is the same—with one move you attack two of your opponent's pieces simultaneously. His losses, the havoc suffered by his defending forces, and your interference with his overall strategic concept can spell his ultimate defeat.

In this position, Black, who has put off castling, is vulnerable to a serious double attack that should cost him the game. Reasoning it more important to develop his Knight than to remove his King to safety, he has just played 1. . . . N-R3, and left himself open to the following:

2. NxN	PxN
3. BxP ch.	K-B
4. BxR	

Thus, White has won a Rook and a pawn, giving him an overwhelming advantage.

Even the pawn can humble a monarch.

Diagram 50

White is down a piece, but his King is safe and the Black King is exposed in the center of the board where he and his Rook can both be attacked by

| 1. P-B6 ch. | K-B |
| 2. PxR ch. | |

And White has more than equalized.

45

Or consider the predicament that Black faced in Diagram 51.

Diagram 51

Again, he has neglected to safeguard his King and deploy his pieces effectively. He has also courted disaster by allowing his King and Queen to be lined up so that they are vulnerable to

1. R-Q7 ch.

The Queen is lost, for even after 1. ... QxR, the White back-up Rook captures the Queen.

Closely related to these attacks are Bishop and Rook checks that force a King to move and then expose to capture another piece on the same rank, file, or diagonal. In this position:

Diagram 52

The White Bishop can check the Black King with 1. B-B4 ch. The Black King must move and then White picks up the Black Rook. The same principle, but with a Rook wielding the broadsword, is shown in:

Diagram 53

Here the Black King and Queen are lined up, always a very precarious position, and the White Rook swoops in for the kill with

1. R-B7 ch.   K moves
2. RxQ

Of course, the checking piece does not have to be a Rook or Bishop as in the above examples. Frequently, a Queen plays the same role. And the shielding piece, here both times the Black King, could be, say, a Queen, as in Diagram 54:

Diagram 54

White can attack the Black Queen and, indirectly, the Black Rook with

1. B-B4

When the Queen retreats, the Rook is captured.

The common denominator in all of these positions is the superior value of the piece that is put in jeopardy, so that it must move and allow the piece behind it to fall.

KNIGHT FORKS

Knight forks are in a special class by themselves; leaping over other pieces, the Knight's sudden appearance "behind the lines" has all the qualities of a cavalry sortie by Jeb Stuart, and is just about as hard to guard against. In the position below, the Black King and Queen must feel reasonably secure behind their wall of pawns and pieces, but the stage is set for a daring pre-dawn raid.

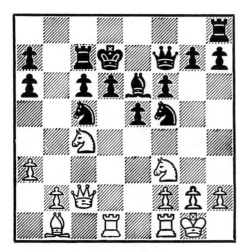

Diagram 55

1. N(4)xP ch!	PxN
2. NxP ch.	K-K2
3. NxQ	KxN

White has won the Queen and two pawns for two Knights—a coup, incidentally, possible only because of the pin of the pawn to the King by the White Rook on the Queen square. If the pin had not been in effect, the second Knight could also have been cap-

tured and White's attack would have failed. Now, set up the position again, but this time place the White Queen Rook on the King's square and see what the sequence of moves might be under these circumstances. With this second position an interesting combination might start with 1. RxP! Even with careful defense, Black comes out behind in material.

Knights have such restless mobility that they must be kept under constant surveillance. At the same time, it is wise to familiarize yourself with their potentialities, so that you can use them in conjunction with your other pieces in ways beyond their individual capacities.

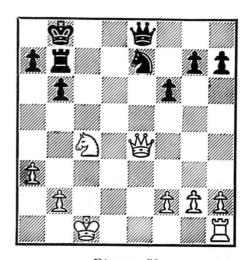

Diagram 56

In this position a forking move by the White Knight, 1. N-Q6, attacking the Queen and the Rook at the same time, fails to accomplish anything after Black moves his Rook to B2, thereby checking White's King and then using his next move to place his Queen on a safe square. But White has other things in mind, for if the Black King and Queen can be attacked by the Knight at the same time:

| 1. QxR ch.! | KxQ |

and now

2. N-Q6 ch.

Thus getting the Queen back and coming out a Rook to the good!

Double attacks and forks work best when the King is one of the pieces attacked. The reason for this is clear—the rules of chess demand that immediate steps be taken to safeguard the royal person, this has top priority, and the well-being of the other endangered piece must be momentarily shelved. And in this crucial moment, before the drawbridge can be raised, the raiding party strikes a devastating blow.

DISCOVERED CHECK

Imagine for a moment, how difficult your defense would be if suddenly, in the middle of the game, your opponent was entitled to one free move with which he could do almost anything! Think of how much damage you could wreak if you, rather than he, had that extra move. This is really what discovered checks can amount to; the effectiveness of this free move is determined by the mobility and striking power of the piece making the move. Take this position:

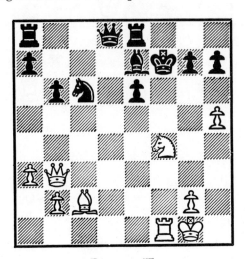

Diagram 57

As soon as the White Knight moves, the Black King is exposed to a check from the Rook, and, of course, must be immediately safeguarded. Meanwhile the Knight can continue his rampage for one more move. If, for example, White plays

| 1. NxP dis. ch. | K-N |
| 2. NxQ dis. ch. | |

then Black loses quickly. Actually, there is a pretty combination in this position known as the "Smothered Mate," made famous years ago. Take a moment and play it through. After Black played

| 2. . . . | K-R |

White continues with

3. N-B7 ch.	K-N
	(forced)
4. N-R6 dbl. ch.	K-R

(Notice this is a double check—a check by both the Queen and the ~~Rook~~ at the same time, so the King must move. There is no way *both* checking pieces can be captured at once, and there is no way a shielding piece can be interposed.)

5. Q-N8 ch.!!	RxQ
(forced)	
6. N-B7 mate!	

The Black King is smothered by his own pieces and has no square to escape to. Since the White Knight cannot be captured, the King is mated!

White is faced with the prospect of losing his Queen Bishop in this position:

AMORY

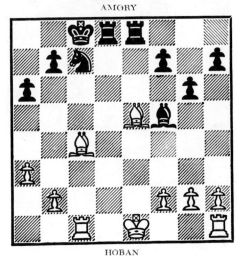

HOBAN

Diagram 58

Pinned to the White King by the Rook on the King square, it cannot be saved by P-

B4, because Black can promptly attack it again with P-B3, nailing tight the coffin lid. But White plays

1. B-K6 ch.!	RxB
2. RxN ch.	K-N
3. R-K7 dis. ch.!	K-R
4. RxR	BxR

And in the game from which this example was taken, White went on to win because his King, being in the center of the board, was more favorably placed for the end-game campaign to Queen a pawn.

DOUBLE CHECK

More deadly than a discovered check, the King is forced to move because it is impossible to capture the two checking pieces at once.

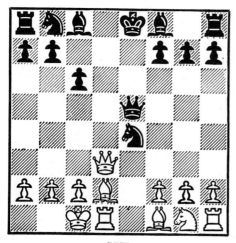

Diagram 59

This position is from a famous game between Richard Reti and Savielly Tartakower, two great masters of the first half of this century.

1. Q-Q8 ch.!!	KxQ
2. B-N5 dbl. ch.	K-B2
(or 2. ... K-K; 3. R-Q8 mate.)	
3. B-Q8 mate!	

But what if the King cannot move? Then he is checkmated as in this game:

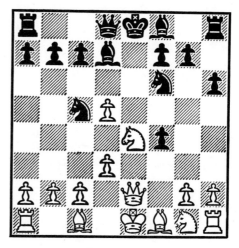

Diagram 60

1. N-Q6 mate

or

1. NxN mate

Frequently, this is written as 1. N-Q6 dble. ch. and mate.

DEFLECTION

This is a tactic that sometimes can be used to deflect or draw away a defender, so that the piece or position it guards is vulnerable.

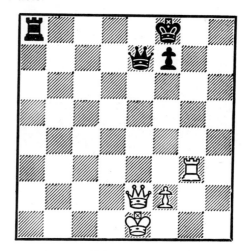

Diagram 61

Both the White and Black Queens are under attack (from each other) and each one is protected only by the King. If the King can be lured or forced away, his Queen falls. White can play

1. R-N8 ch.!   KxR
2. QxQ

But if Black has the move, then

1. . . .   R-R8 ch.
2. K-Q2   R-R7 ch.
3. K moves   QxQ

Diagram 62

Here with 1. B-Q8 ch., the Black King is

forced away from his QB2 and White can capture the Queen.

Diagram 63

In Diagram 63, the Black Queen is fully occupied in preventing her liege lord from being mated at KN2. With 1. B-N4, White is able to deflect the Queen, since her only escape is 1. . . . QxB, and force checkmate.

When you play over the games in the games section you will find many variations on these themes. Search for them in every position—as Marshall did in his brilliant defense against Marco's almost sure win (see page 67).

THE STAGES OF A CHESS GAME

THE STAGES OF A CHESS GAME

WHEN A NATION WAGES WAR, it passes through several stages which merge, almost imperceptibly, with each other, but all of which are important parts in the overall strategic plan. The logic of chess follows this pattern closely. Even the advent of intercontinental ballistic missiles and hydrogen warheads has not changed these logical sequences; they have merely speeded them up. At the first sign of danger, mobilization is ordered and the armed forces are strengthened and deployed. Then the assault against the enemy's strongpoints commences. His territory is invaded, his lines of communication cut, his troop concentrations attacked, and a major effort is directed against the vital heartland—in feudal days against the enemy capital and King's main fortress, in more modern times against the source of industrial power and war-making capacity. During these attacks, defenses, and counterattacks, the outcome may be in doubt. Successful skirmishes and ambuscades are counterbalanced by routs and major or minor disasters in other parts of the war theater.

Then, as the smoke of battle clears away, the pattern of victory and/or defeat emerges. The side that has obtained an advantage, either material or positional, moves in to mop up the last pockets of resistance and apply the final, killing stroke.

Chess games have an opening phase in which each side develops its pieces, deploying them for maximum effectiveness in the attack against the enemy. At the same time the homeland defenses are looked to. This is usually accomplished in the first ten to fifteen moves of the game.

The middle game sees the battle fought with its greatest intensity. Fierce sorties are met with heroic counterattacks and sacrifices. Redoubts are besieged, fortified walls battered and breached, then repaired in desperate haste. Reserves are rushed to the points of greatest danger. This stage can last for ten to thirty moves or more, and, unless a decision is reached, leads to the end game.

In the end game, most of the pieces are off the board, victims of the ferocious carnage of the middle game. The Kings can safely enter the battlefield and they do so, ponderously and magnificently, to bully the hostile pawns and support their own in the struggle to reach the eighth rank. Here, a pawn can be promoted to Queen or other piece (except a King). These fresh troops shift and influence the tide of battle.

Or perhaps the situation dicates a different strategy; for example, the King may support his last remaining army units in their hunt to annihilate the fleeting and abandoned adversary-King. An end-game phase can last for as long as forty or fifty moves, depending on the resourcefulness of the defense.

All of the above should be considered broad strokes on the canvas, for there are as many exceptions as there are rules and axioms. In Chapter III, we saw a game only seven moves long, not even the length of the usual opening. We presented it to you because it demonstrates some of the excitement and vitality of chess, and because it shows how an error in planning basic strategy can be fatal at any point in the game. White always has the first move, and therefore White always starts out with the initiative. White's objective is to keep this initiative and drive home a successful attack. Black's effort is to equalize, blunt the attack, seize the initiative, and launch a successful counterattack. This, then, is the essential conflict in every opening and middle game. Its resolution sets the stage for the final phase.

At the beginning of Chapter V, when we discussed some of the distinctions between strategy and tactics, we considered the factors that influence opening principles. Over the years, all sorts of immutable rules have been proposed—"Do not move any pawns in the opening of a game but the K and Q pawns"; "Do not move any piece twice in the opening"; "Develop the Knights before the Bishops, especially the QB," etc. Over the years these have become more and more mutable. Even the great Lasker succumbed to temptation. Yet, not long after, Nimzowitsch, Reti, and Alekhine came along and defeated the leaders of the old school by disregarding its precepts and substituting new ones. The old rigidities went by the board,

and new dogmas took over. What, then, are we to use as guides?

First, I would suggest flexibility. Examine every rule from the point of view of logic and rationality. Does it make sense and is it pragmatic? Are there overriding considerations that make it necessary to suspend, for the moment, even good rules? I would suggest that you examine the reasoning behind these rules, so that you can determine for yourself when they should or should not be followed.

For example, consider the problem of development. Since you and your opponent have the same number of pieces and the same number of moves, it seems reasonable to assume that the side executing its moves most efficiently (that is, positioning its pieces judiciously for attack and defense in the shortest possible time) will enter the middle game with an advantage. Again, the side that sees its King safely castled would seem to have a better chance for defending it and launching an attack. It has no need to be concerned about the safety of its own monarch, or to parry assaults and threats against an exposed King. Castling has the additional advantage of getting a Rook into the center of the board, usually to work with the other Rook.

In this spirit, then, I am going to suggest guidelines that should help you in formulating an overall strategy and executing tactics. Every guideline may be violated, suspended, bent, broken, or warped *if you have good and compelling reasons to do so.* In the absence of a good and compelling reason, however, don't be iconoclastic solely for the sake of opposing the establishment.

Since the opening involves a struggle for the control of the center and most martially active part of the chessboard, as you develop your pieces *deploy them toward the center, or so that they bear upon the center* (thus, a Bishop on N2 strikes at this heartland). Develop your Knights first and place them on squares (KB3 and QB3 are generally best) where they will have maximum attacking and defending scope. Develop your Bishops next, and try to refrain from pinning the adverse Knights before your opponent has castled.

Generally speaking, it is usually unwise to bring out your Queen and Rooks prematurely since this will subject them to harassing attacks from Knights, Bishops, and pawns and force you to lose tempi. And, as we've said, tend to your King and its safe castling before your opponent can prevent it. Conversely, try to prevent your opponent from castling.

Usually, the fewer pawn moves executed in the beginning the better. Some experts go so far to maintain that pawns should only be moved to free the pieces locked behind them. Doubled pawns (that is, pawns on the same file and of the same color) unquestionably create weaknesses, since they cannot support each other. Holes in the pawn structure are created when pawns of the same color are on different ranks. This is another form of weakness, since hostile pieces can then occupy these squares and may be difficult to dislodge. Adolph Anderssen, a great player of the nineteenth century, once remarked that if you could get one of your Knights posted on the fifth or sixth rank, your game "would play itself!" He must have had a phobia about Knights because he also once observed that "a Knight on the sixth rank is like a rusty nail in the knee."

Because the pawn structure will be important to the end game, it is vital not to let poor moves in the opening and middle game weaken it; as we shall see, games are frequently decided in the end by the relative weaknesses or strengths in the pawn positions. Remember, since pawns can never move back, every pawn move is irrevocable and a pawn weakness, once created, will remain like an albatross hanging from your neck.

As there is a subtle transition between the opening and the middle game (even Grand Masters would disagree as to the demarkation), so there is a subtle blending of principles of play in the two stages. Some of the principles used in the opening and discussed above apply to the middle game, but to a lesser extent. New concepts are introduced and new dynamics evolve. Now it is important to get the Rooks into play and to place them on open files. (An open file is one which is unobstructed by pawns.) Cramped positions should be avoided and your pieces, now completely developed, should be kept mobile. After all, the superior strength of the Queen is irrelevant if she cannot be where you need her in time to attack or defend. The might of the British Navy was useless to the defense of Singapore when the Japanese attacked through the jungle.

Avoid blocking the mobility of your Bishops with your own pawns. In chess parlance such a blocked Bishop is referred to as a bad Bishop and can be the equivalent of playing a piece down. The observations we made about pawns still have validity in the middle game—holes should be avoided, as should the doubling up of the pawns. As a matter of fact, it is a good idea to acquire the habit of considering the effect of any pawn move you make on the end game *before* you make it!

Whereas the middle game abounds in combinations and sacrifices, the end game is frequently distilled down to the conversion of just one pawn into a win. Here the role of the King becomes a dominating theme. The side with the pawn advantage works to simplify, that is, to get rid, through exchange of the opposing pieces so that the pawn can be promoted to the eighth rank. Then, when *it* becomes a Queen (this is the usual case, although a Rook, Bishop, or Knight may also be chosen), the enemy is usually routed quickly.

Since end-game technique is much more precise, the axioms governing it have been tested out in countless games of tournament play and analysis and have more validity. The side with a passed pawn should advance it as rapidly as possible, while ensuring that it can be supported when deep in enemy territory. Rooks should be kept *behind* the passed pawn. In this way, your own Rook behind your own passed pawn can protect it up to the eighth rank and prevent an opposition Rook from attacking the pawn in the rear. Passed pawns should be blockaded by the King. The side with a one- or two-pawn advantage should exchange pieces, but not pawns, and the side behind in pawns should try to retain all its pieces and exchange as many pawns as possible.

All the principles we've discussed apply in varying degrees to all the stages of a chess game. Some have more significance at one stage; some have a general application. For example, never move without considering what your opponent's replies might be. And every time your opponent moves ask yourself what he threatens. It is always wise to avoid giving useless checks to the other King; frequently when this occurs you help your adversary repair his position or remove his King to a safer sanctuary. At the same time, you waste valuable time and neglect to execute a carefully thought-out and systematic plan of attack.

Last, always assume that your opponent will move correctly. Yes, set traps, but do not count on blunders. Make your every move a threat, while still pursuing basic objectives.

Does all this sound like too much? No player applies all the correct principles in every situation or on every move. The important thing is to have an awareness of the basics. Then your game will exhibit steady improvement, you will derive much more from your over-the-board analysis, and the games of the masters and champions will make more sense and give you more enjoyment.

In the next chapters we will give examples from master play that illustrate some of the above observations. From here on the order is reversed—end-game positions will be considered first, then middle-game combinations, and then openings. This is based on the assumption that knowledge of what the end-game objectives are will be helpful in determining strategic and tactical ploys in the middle game. After all, there is no point in launching a brilliant combination if the result is a losing end-game position! In turn, a familiarity with the kinds of positions leading to winning combinations is essential to the proper handling of the openings.

THE
END
GAME

THE END GAME

ACCORDING TO JOSEF STALIN, the sweetest experience he "ever had was slipping between clean, cool sheets at the end of a hard day spent slaking revenge on his enemies!" Maybe this was because he never played a good end game. If he had, many poor souls might have been spared much anguish. The position you find yourself in when the last stage of the game begins is the reward or penalty for everything you have done in the opening and the middle game. If you have developed a plan, executed it logically and efficiently, made few mistakes and exploited those of your opponent, then you are about to reap the rewards. And, of course, there is the opposite side of the coin. If you have bumbled through the opening and fumbled through the middle game, the chances are that your adversary is about to do some slaking of his own. Being optimistic, we're going to approach this as though we have the material or space superiority necessary to win. But consider carefully all of the defensive maneuverings of the weaker side. Sometimes careful defense can result in a draw

and you should be familiar with these artful dodges.

The end game begins when most of the pieces have been cleared off the board. Now the King comes into his own. No longer forced to remain in his castle-keep, he can (and should) enter the lists as a champion. Assuming an active role on the battlefield, he can lead his remaining forces in a King hunt—the checkmate of the rival monarch. If the remaining resources of the enemy prevent this, or if the pieces at hand are insufficient to force checkmate, it may be possible to promote a pawn to the eighth rank, "Queening" it, and then using this additional strength to hammer home the winning attack. How many times on a real battlefield have two decimated and exhausted forces faced each other, neither having sufficient remaining strength to deliver the bold and final stroke. Suddenly, in the distance, the sound of a fresh bugle—the reserves have arrived!

Consider the positions in Diagram 64.

Each exhibits a Queen mate. In every instance you will notice that the active coop-

59

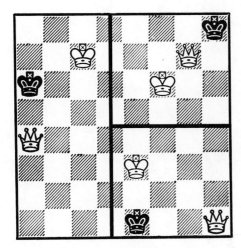

Diagram 64

1. Q-R4	K-Q4
2. K-Q2	K-B4
3. K-B3	K-N4
4. Q-B4 ch.	K-N3
5. K-N4	K-N2
6. K-N5	K-R2

Here, as in all Queen mates, White must guard carefully against a stalemate (7.Q-QB7 ch., K-R; 8.K-N6 stalemate!)

7. Q-KB7 ch.	K-N
8. K-N6	K-R or K-B
9. Q-K8 mate	

MATE WITH A KING AND A ROOK VERSUS A KING

There are similarities in this mate with the one just discussed. Again, the hunted King must be driven to the edge of the board. And again the White King must help his Rook. To limit Black's mobility, White plays:

eration of the White King is essential. It is also essential to drive the Black King to the edge of the board. *Unless there are other pieces or pawns present, the King cannot be mated in the center.* If the Black King is in the center, as in Diagram 65:

Diagram 65

Diagram 66

White's first step is to limit his mobility by putting his Queen on, say, R4 (B6 is just as good). With this one move, the Black King is confined to less than one half the board! Then the White King is moved forward to support the Queen and the free terrain left to the hunted King becomes even smaller. The sequence of moves might go something like this:

1. R-R7	K-B
2. K-B2	K-N
3. R-R7	K-B
4. K-K3	K-K
5. K-Q4	K-Q
6. K-B5	K-B
7. K-B6	K-N
8. R-R7	K-R

(If 8. . . . K-B, then 9. R-R8 mate.)

9.	K-N6	K-N
10.	R-R8 mate	

But what if the Black King occupies the center of the board? The same basic technique is used. The White King is brought up so that it opposes the Black King on the same file, then a Rook check forces the King back one rank, and back again, until it is against the edge of the board and cannot retreat further. Then the *coup de grâce* is administered.

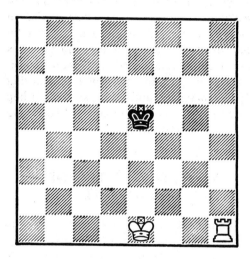

Diagram 67

1.	R-R4	K-B4
2.	K-B2	K-N4
3.	R-R4	K-B4
4.	K-K3	

Now if 4. . . . K-K4; 5. R-R5 ch. and the Black King must retreat one rank. Black tries to avoid the inevitable for as long as possible, and plays

4.	. . .	K-N4
5.	K-B3	K-R4
6.	K-N3	K-N4
7.	R-R5 ch.	K-B3
8.	K-B4	K-N3

Now White must make a stalling move with his Rook. If, instead, he moves his King to N4, the Black King moves to B3, and a check by the Rook allows the Black King to slip out at K4. Hence

9.	R-QN5	K-R3
10.	K-N4	K-N3
11.	R-N6 ch.	K-B2

And so forth, driving the king to his first rank and mate.

MATE WITH TWO ROOKS

If White's skillful earlier play enabled him to accumulate a surplus of two Rooks, the active participation of the White King is not required. The two Rooks can mate by acting in tandem:

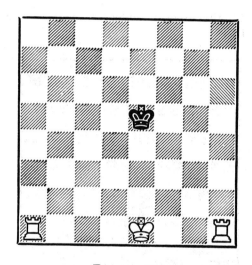

Diagram 68

1.	R-KR4	K-B4
2.	R-QR5 ch.	K-N3
3.	KR-QN4	K-B3
4.	R-N6 ch.	K-K2
5.	R-R7 ch.	K-Q
6.	R-N7 mate	

MATE WITH TWO BISHOPS

Two Bishops, working together, form an impenetrable barrier that the opposing King cannot cross. The mate must take place in the corner with the active assistance of the White King. Diagram 69 shows two mating patterns:

Diagram 69

Starting from a random position such as this:

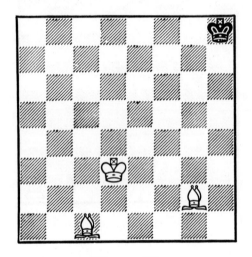

Diagram 70

White can play

1. B-K4	K-N2
2. B-N5	K-B2
3. B-B5	

The Black King is limited to six squares.

| 3. . . . | K-N2 |

Now the White King advances ominously. . . .

4. K-K4	K-B2
5. K-K5	K-N2
6. K-K6	K-B

7. B-B6	K-K
8. B-N6 ch.	K-B
9. B-Q4	K-N
10. K-B6	K-B

If 10. . . . K-R; 11.K-B7 discovered mate.

11. B-B5 ch.	K-N
12. B-K4	K-R
13. K-N6	K-N
14. B-Q5 ch.	K-R
15. B-Q4 mate	

Aside from remembering that the King must be mated in the corner, *always make sure that he has a square to go to or that you are checking him on the move.* This is vital; a stalemate is a constant menace and exactly what Black is struggling for. Practice this mate from several different random positions and acquire the habit of (1) guarding against stalemate and (2) using a Bishop move to gain time and force the Black King to a less desirable square.

MATE WITH A BISHOP AND KNIGHT

This mate is too difficult and complex to discuss effectively here. This much can be said, however: the mate must take place in the corner of the board that is the same color as the squares on which the Bishop moves. The mating positions are shown in diagram 71.

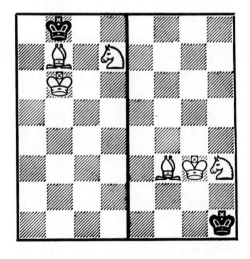

Diagram 71

KING AND PAWN ENDINGS

Until now the pawn has been like the dormouse in Alice's *Adventures in Wonderland*—suppressed. In the opening it was pretty much in the way of its own pieces. In the middle game it was used to assault the enemy fortifications and was thrown into the breach with little regard for its well-being. But now in the end it comes into its own. One pawn can mean the difference between victory and defeat. One pawn, promoted to the eighth rank, becomes an all-powerful Queen, or a Rook, Bishop, or Knight. And the closer the pawn advances to the eighth rank the more of a menace it becomes to the other side. More and more attention must be devoted to it. Valuable pieces—Rooks, Bishops, or Knights—and sometimes even the Queen, must devote their energies to controlling the pesky interloper and preventing it from reaching pawn nirvana. Of course, if an advancing pawn is opposed by one or more hostile pawns, its threatening potential is small. But if there are no pawns that can stop it, if it is a passed pawn, then its mere presence can make Kings quake, Queens scurry, and Bishops cross themselves. The passed pawn becomes even more of a menace as pieces are exchanged. Now the Kings are at their most effective. Immune from each other, they attack blockading pawns and try to guide their own through the opposition mine fields, pitfalls, and ambuscades.

In Chapter II we considered the significance of the opposition and its value in a simple pawn ending. Actually it is a deciding factor in most King and pawn endings when there are no other pieces on the board, because it can be decisive in determining the mobility and effectiveness of the Kings.

A good general rule to remember is that *when two Kings are facing each other, no matter how far apart, on the same line, and the number of squares between them is even, the King having the move can seize the opposition.*

Here, whoever has the move wins, as long as the opposition is not lost.

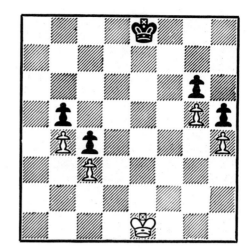

Diagram 72

1. K-K2	K-K2
2. K-K3	K-K3
3. K-K4	K-Q3
4. K-Q4	K-B3
5. K-K5	K-B2
6. K-Q5	K-N3
7. K-Q6	K-N2
8. K-B5	K-R3

9. K-B6 and the Black pawns must fall.

Black made a valiant effort to support his forces, but could not overcome White's greater mobility. Now consider the same position with Black having the move:

1. . . .	K-K2
2. K-K2	K-K3
3. K-K3	K-K4!
4. K-B3	K-B4
5. K-N3	K-K5

The White pawns must be captured. In both of these situations, as soon as the blockading pawns fall the pawns they barred can press forward to Queen.

Consider the pawns in diagram 73. Here, since the Kings are out of action for all practical purposes, White must devise a strategy for breaking through the Black pawn guard.

1. P-N5!	BPxP
2. P-R5!	PxRP
3. P-B5 To become a Queen.	

Diagram 73

Then White won't have any trouble picking up the remaining pawns before they can reach their Queening rank. But notice how the situation would be changed if the Black King had been posted at KN3 instead of KR3!

Diagram 74

3. . . .	K-B3
4. P-B6	K-K3
5. P-B7	K-Q2

And the unsupported pawn swings over the gallows' trap as the courier with the King's pardon gallops down the road. A valuable rule of thumb is illustrated in this ending. Draw an imaginary diagonal from the pawn to the eighth rank. Then build this into a square. If the opposition King can move into this square, he can stop the pawn from Queening. If he is already in this area *and it is White's move*, Black still stops the pawn. An exception to this rule occurs when the pawn has not made its first move. Since it can move two squares initially, the diagonal must take this fact into account and be drawn from the square in front of the pawn. Set up various pawn positions such as you might run into in the end game and play them out. You will find that they can be figured with great accuracy and precision.

For instance, where the White King is behind his pawn as here:

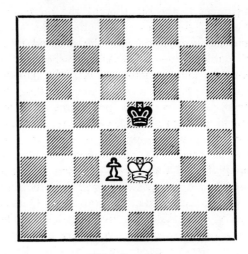

Diagram 75

Black is able to draw by *keeping the opposition*. It may not seem from the diagram that the White King is behind his pawn, but that's where he ends up with either

1. P-Q4 ch.	K-Q4

or

1. K-B3	K-Q5
2. K-K2	

The reason that this position ends in a draw is that White must either give up the pawn or stalemate the Black King. The sequence might go like this:

1. P-Q4 ch.	K-Q4
2. K-Q3	K-Q3
3. K-K4	K-K3
(always keeping the opposition)	

4. P-Q5 ch.	K-Q3
5. K-Q4	K-Q2
6. K-K5	K-K2
7. P-Q6 ch.	K-Q2
8. K-Q5	K-Q
9. K-K6	K-K
10. P-Q7 ch.	K-Q
11. K-Q6 stalemate.	

But if the White King is two or more squares in front of his pawn, White always wins because he can use a pawn move at the right time to hold the opposition. (This two-square rule does not apply when the pawn is a Rook pawn. In that case, if the Black King can get to the R, N, or B squares, he can draw.)

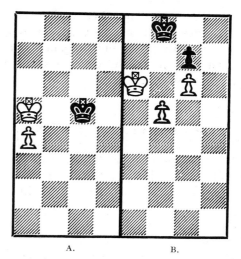

Diagram 76

1. P-K3	K-B3
2. K-Q5	K-K2
3. K-K5	K-B2
4. K-Q6	K-B3
5. P-K4	K-B2
6. P-K5	K-K
7. K-K6	K-B
8. K-Q7; the Pawn marches in.	

Another important end-game position to be familiar with involves the Rook pawn and opposition. If the White King is in front of his pawn, on the Rook file and the Black King has the opposition, he can keep the White King locked in, blocking his own pawn, or the Black King can reach the Rook square and draw. (Diagram 77-A.).

Diagram 77

1. K-R6	K-B3
2. K-R7	K-B2
3. P-R5	K-B
4. P-R6	K-B2
5. K-R	K-B
6. P-R7	K-B2

Stalemate.

Every end-game pawn position should be very carefully analyzed and all its potentialities explored. Possibilities abound in even the most obvious situations. Consider Diagram 77-B. Here White is a pawn ahead, but if he tries to bludgeon his rival with P-B6, Black can force a draw:

1. P-B6	K-N!
2. PxP	KxP draw
or	
2. P-B7 ch.	K-B draw

But White has a better tactic at hand—the rapier!

1. K-Q7	K-N
2. K-K7	K-R
3. P-B6	PxP
(if 3. . . . K-N; 4. P-B7 ch., K-R; 5. P-B8 (Q) mate)	
4. K-B7!	P-B4
5. P-N7 ch.	K-R2
6. P-N8 (Q) ch.	K-R3
7. Q-N6 mate	

Obviously there are many more King and pawn endings. Familiarity with the advantages and disadvantages inherent in them guides the moves you elect in the middle game. After all, there is no point, for example, to simplify in the middle game by exchanging, if the pawn structure spells an end-game loss.

QUEEN VERSUS PAWN

What happens if you Queen your pawn first, but Black has a pawn on the homestretch, protected by the King? Your King is somewhere on the other side of the Board, where he has been involved in an independent excursion of his own, and cannot possibly get to where the action is unless he can make a forced march.

Diagram 78

With accurate Queen tactics, the Black King can be forced to waste moves, and every time he does the White King can slip closer.

1. Q-K5 ch.		K-B7
2. Q-Q4 ch.		K-K7
3. Q-K4 ch.		K-B7
4. Q-Q3		K-K8
5. Q-K3 ch.		K-Q8

This is the key position; now the White King has a free move, while Black must waste time moving out of the way of his own pawn.

6. K-B6		K-B7
7. Q-K2		K-B8
8. Q-B4 ch.		K-N7

9. Q-Q3		K-B8
10. Q-B3 ch.		K-Q8
11. K-K5		K-K7
12. Q-B2		K-K8
13. Q-K4 ch.		K-B7
14. Q-Q3		K-K8
15. Q-K3 ch.		K-Q8
16. K-Q4		K-B7
17. Q-B3 ch.		K-Q8
18. K-Q3		K-K8
19. QxP ch.—with a quick mate in the offing!		

But be careful where you place your King as he races across the desolate battlefield to join in the fight. If he gets in the way of his Queen and prevents her from harassing the Black King, you may end up with a draw. This technique will not work where the pawn involved is a BP or an RP. In these situations, Black can achieve a stalemate by getting to R8.

KING AND QUEEN AGAINST KING AND ROOK

This is a hard struggle. The Queen enjoys greater mobility, but the Rook has a vicious punch and if White lets his guard down the Black Rook can wreak havoc. The key to White's attack is to force the Black King and Rook to separate so that the Queen can check the King and the Rook at the same time, winning the Rook. In this position:

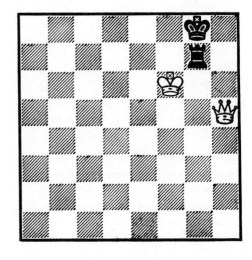

Diagram 79

If it is Black's move he is in trouble. He must move his Rook away from his King and then it will fall to the double-check motif. (If he moves his King to the B square, Q-R6 pins the Rook and Black loses immediately.)

1. . . .	R-N6
2. Q-Q5 ch.	

And now Black is in a dilemma: if 2. . . . K-B; 3. Q-Q8 mate. If 2. . . . K-R; 3. Q-R8 ch., R-N; 4. Q-R mate, and if 2. . . . K-R2; 3. Q-K4 ch., K-N; 4. Q-B4 ch., K-R; 5. Q-R4 ch. and winning the Rook!

But what if it is not Black's move in this position? *Then White should create the identical position with Black having to move.* Here's how:

1. Q-Q5 ch.	K-R
2. Q-R ch.	K-N (R-R2;
	3. Q-R8 mate)
3. Q-R5	

And now Black must follow the unfortunate direction mentioned above.

The same general principle applies when a King and a Rook are pitted against a King and a Bishop. This results in a draw *most* of the time. But if the King and the Bishop can be separated, White has a good chance of winning. In the following position, White has a clear course of action.

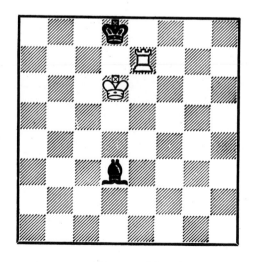

Diagram 80

With

1. R-K3	B-B4
2. R-KB3	B-Q2
3. R-B8 ch.	B-K
and	
4. R-R8	K-B, (forced!)
deserting the Bishop	

Most of the time White must swallow his pride and settle for a draw. The main value in discussing this at all is to drive home the point that every position abounds in mystery and hidden tactical and strategic possibilities that can reward perceptive generalship. Sometimes even an apparent loss can be saved by imagination.

One of the most amazing end games on record started with this position. The American master, Frank Marshall, was playing Georg Marco of Austria and suddenly found that Black's careful strategy had forced a pawn to the sixth rank. A critical moment had been reached. The invasion deep into White territory threatened imminent disaster.

Position after Black's Forty-fourth Move

MARCO

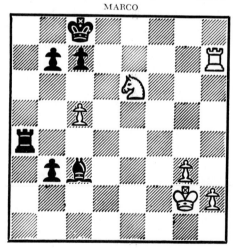

MARSHALL
Monte Carlo, 1904
Diagram 81

Marshall thought long and hard, and then—

45. P-B6!

Avoiding the trap 45. RxP ch., K-N, winning.

45. ...	B-K4

If 45. .... PxP, then White has all sorts of drawing chances. Consider this sequence: 46. RxP ch., K-N; 47. R-N7 ch.! KxR; 48. N-B5 ch.! K-B2; 49. NxR and prevents the pawn from Queening. Or 47. RxP, R-R7 ch.; 48. K-B3, P-N7; 49. R-N6 ch., K-R2; 50. R-N3 or 50. RxP with good drawing chances.

No.	White	Black
46.	PxP ch.	K-N
47.	N-B5	R-R7 ch.
48.	K-R3	P-N7
49.	R-K7!	K-R2
50.	R-K8	P-B3
51.	R-R8 ch.	K-N3
52.	RxR	P-N8 (Queen)
53.	P-N8 (Queen) ch.!!	BxQ
54.	R-N2 ch.	QxR
55.	N-R4 ch.	K-N4
56.	NxQ	P-B4
57.	K-N2	P-B5
58.	K-B3	P-B6
59.	N-Q3	K-B5
60.	N-K	K-Q4
61.	P-R4	B-Q3
62.	P-N4	B-K2
63.	P-N5	K-K4
64.	K-N4	B-B
65.	N-B2	K-K5
66.	P-R5	K-Q6
67.	N-R!	K-K5
68.	P-R6	K-K4
69.	K-R5	K-B4
70.	N-B2	B-Q3
71.	N-Q4 ch.	K-K5
72.	N-K2	P-B7
73.	P-N6	B-R6
74.	P-N7	K-Q6
75.	P-N8 (Queen)	KxN
76.	Q-R2	Resigns

"Time, you thief, who love to get sweets into your list, put that in!"

68

8.

THE
MIDDLE
GAME

THE MIDDLE GAME

IF THE OPENING SETS THE STAGE for the attack, the middle game sees it launched and brought to its greatest intensity. Ideally, each side has developed its pieces in favorable positions and is now ready for this supreme test. When the strategic plan of one side is markedly successful, the game may end abruptly with a sudden checkmate or such a drastic decimation of the enemy defenders that further resistance is pointless. Or, as we have seen, it may transpose into the end game with the outcome still in doubt. In such an event, the slightest advantages should be carefully nurtured; they may be sufficient to tilt the scales for victory.

How is a strategic plan best carried out? The soundest positional moves are made, that is, moves that place pieces where they can work together well and not get in each other's way. Each side feints and probes, hoping to find or create weaknesses in the enemy defenses. Minute advantages of space, material, and tempi are accumulated, husbanded for the grand assault. When one side feels that it has sufficient superiority to launch an attack, it concentrates on the opponent's weakest points, the most difficult squares to defend. Then comes the all-out effort to win a decisive advantage.

Capablanca put it succinctly: "Once the opportunity is offered, all the pieces are thrown into action *en masse* when necessary; then they coordinate their action smoothly and with machinelike precision."

This sequence of moves is called a combination and is actually a tactical operation on a grand scale. The combination may be to end the game through checkmate, or through the capture of substantial material, or to achieve a winning end-game position. For example, an end-game position where one side can force a pawn through to the eighth rank and then, with this additional Queen, silence the last pockets of resistance. Or the combination may be of more modest design with the ultimate objective of winning a smaller advantage—a pawn, some terrain, or the dislocation of the hostile troops. If such is the case, further tactical operations may become necessary to capitalize on the potential of these gains.

Let us look at some of these combinations, to get a feel for them, and begin to understand how they embody the very essence of chess. A beautifully conceived and executed combination can be a work of art, as much a product of genius as is great music or great painting.

will have an overall plan and a concept of the pattern he intends to follow. The following was taken from a game by Alexander Alekhine, who was to defeat Capablanca and become World Champion a few years later.

U.S.S.R., 1950
KUSMINICH

TAIMANOV
Diagram 82

Paris, 1913
PRAT

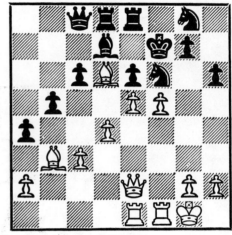

ALEKHINE
Diagram 83

1. Q-R5 ch.!!	NxQ
2. PxP dbl. ch.	K-N3
3. B-B2 ch.	K-N4
4. R-B5 ch.	K-N3
5. R-B6 dbl. ch.	K-N4
6. R-N6 ch.	K-R5
7. R-K4 ch.	N-B5
8. RxN ch.	K-R4
9. P-N3 and there is no move Black can make that will prevent the 10. R-R4 mate that is coming up!	

Study Diagram 82 for a moment. Black has a slight advantage in material; White controls more territory. Black looks secure with two commanding Bishops and a well-placed Knight, when suddenly—

1. N-N6!!

This threatens 2. Q-R8 mate, and if 1. ... PxN; 2. BxB ch. and winning the Queen. So Black plays

1. ...	N-R2
2. RxB!	PxR
3. QxR! ch.	QxQ
4. BxP mate!	

Some combinations may be quite long, but are all of a piece, that is, they have a consistent unity and logic that gives them coherence. At the outset, the player may not see the exact moves he will make, but he

This next *tour de force* was played by George Koltanowski—*while blindfolded!*

1. BxP ch.!	KxB
2. Q-R5 ch.	K-N
3. BxP	KxB
4. Q-N5 ch.	K-R
5. R-Q4	B-R7 ch.
6. K-R	Q-B5
7. RxQ	BxR
8. QxB	R-KN
9. R-K5	Resigns

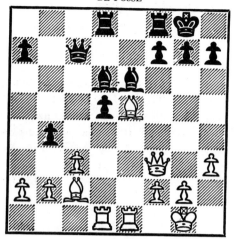

Gent, 1936
DE FOSSE

KOLTANOWSKI
(BLINDFOLDED)

Diagram 84

Here is another Alekhine masterpiece—a brilliant attack that seems to materialize out of thin air. Before we get into the play, let us study the position for a moment.

First Brilliancy Prize Pistyan, 1922
WOLF

ALEKHINE

Diagram 85

The forces on each side are equal: six pawns, two Knights, two Rooks, and a Queen. White has a significant advantage in space, for White's Rooks are "joined" (that

is, they are connected and can work together) while the Black Rooks are separated and have little prospect of ever cooperating. Black's pieces are poorly positioned for either offense or the defense of the King, which is in a vulnerable posture. White's King is safe, and so White's strategic problem is how to convert the plus factors into a winning attack. In typical fashion, this chessboard conjurer strikes:

| 1. RxN! | PxR |
| 2. N-N5 | |

Threatening 3. NxKP ch. and winning the Queen. But what if Black throws in a threat of his own, with 2. ... P-K4? Now if 3. N-K6 ch., K-K; 4. NxQ, PxQ. But White doesn't have to play this sequence. If Black counters with 2. ... P-K4, White first moves his Queen to safety *and at the same time* threatens mate with 3. Q-Q5 (threatening mate on B7).

Black might think that he has an answer with 3. ... Q-K (preventing the mate and avoiding the Knight fork), but 4. N-K6 ch., K-B2; 5. N-B7 dis. ch., P-K3; 6. Q-B3 ch., K-N2; 7. NxQ ch. So Black's best chances lie in

2. ...	Q-N
3. NxKP ch.	K-B2
4. N-N5 ch.	K-B

If the Black King goes to his King square at this point, the remaining White Rook joins the attack with 5. R-K.

5. Q-Q5	R-N2
6. N-K6 ch.	K-N
7. NxR dis. ch.	KxN
8. PxP	N-B3
9. QxP	R-R2
10. R-K	Q-Q3

Trying to force some counter play. But Black is too far behind in pawns and position to have any prospects.

11. P-K8 (taking a Knight instead of a Queen) ch.!	
11. ...	NxN
12. QxN	QxN
13. Q-K5 ch.	K-B2
14. P-KR4	

Bringing up additional force and opening an escape for the White King so that he will not be mated on the eighth rank later on by the Black Queen or Rook—always a wise precaution to take.

14. . . .	RxP!
15. Q-K8 ch.	K-N2
16. R-K7 ch.	K-R3
17. Q-B8 ch.	K-R4
18. R-K5 ch.	K-N5

If the Black King takes the Rook pawn, the White Queen check on R3 leads to mate in short order.

19. R-N5 ch.!

Avoiding Black's last venomous sting. If White had played 19. P-B3 ch., K-N6; 20. R-N5 ch., QxR!!; 21. PxQ, R-R8 mate!

19. . . .   Resigns

This was a superb example of a strategic plan masterfully conceived and executed. But some combinations in the middle game are short and deadly.

New York, 1857
MORPHY

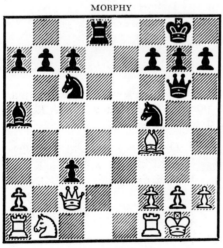

MARACHE
Diagram 86

Paul Morphy, America's first chess genius and strongest player of his day, was in command of the Black pieces. He played

| 1. . . . | N(B3)-Q5 |
| 2. Q-K4 | N-KN6!! |

White's Queen is attacked in two ways—by the Black Knight and Queen—so

3. QxQ   N(Q5)-K7 mate!!

Was this *coup* due to a blunder on White's part in moving his Queen to K4? What other moves are available to White? If 2. Q-Q, P-B7; 3. Q-Q3, N-N6!; 4. QxN, N-K7 ch., and winning the Queen. And even 2. Q-R4 leads to another kind of disaster: 2. . . . P-N4; 3. QxB, N-K7 ch.; 4. K-R, NxB; 5. R-N (to prevent the mate at N7), R-Q8; 6. P-N3, Q-B3 ch.!; 7. P-B3, QxP mate!

This is the kind of beauty that will live as long as there are chess sets and players, as will the following "one mover":

Breslau, 1912
MARSHALL

LEWITZKY
Diagram 87

Both the Black Queen and the Black Rook are attacked. The White King seems secure in his fortress, protected by his Queen and Rook and pawns, but Marshall made a move he described as the most elegant move he ever played. It may well be the most elegant move ever played by any master!

1. . . .   Q-KN6!!!

The Black Queen can be taken in three ways—2. RxQ, or 2. BPxQ, or 2. QxQ—and each is fatal. For example, if RPxQ, N-K7, mate; if BPxQ, N-K7 ch.; 3. K-R, RxR mate, and if QxQ, N-K7 ch.; 3. K-R, NxQ ch.; 4. K-N, NxR, and Black ends up a piece ahead!

Middle-game play may be initiated with one of several objectives in mind. The examples we have just seen were aimed at the capture of the rival King. This is, of course, always the long-range objective in every chess game, but it may not be the immediate purpose of a combination. The main reason we discussed end-game techniques before middle and opening play was to make clear what kind of objectives you should have in mind *before* you formulate your middle-game strategy. Try to acquire the practice of visualizing a winning position that is attainable given the variables you have at hand, and then work out a realistic plan to reach that position. It may almost go without saying that it is important to know how to proceed once you get to your ideal condition—how to win a won game—but this is technique that depends on practice and the development, the constant honing, of your skills.

The position shown in Diagram 88 required just such foresight. Played between Botwinnick, destined to be a great World Champion, and Capablanca, a former great World Champion, it is crisp, clean, logical, and almost scientific—but it still has that thread of gold running through it that bespeaks artistry.

Black has a slight material edge of one pawn, and the control of space is tilted toward White (of course, against former World Champions, don't expect too much). White's Bishop seems out of the action, but White has a passed pawn that drains energy from the Black forces and is tying up the Black Queen. White's objective is clearly to capitalize on this advanced pawn and either Queen it or force Black to pay an inordinately high price for its capture.

1. B-R3!!	QxB
2. N-R5 ch.!	PxN
3. Q-N5 ch.	K-B
4. QxN ch.	K-N

If 4. . . . K-K, 5. Q-B7 ch., K-Q; 6. Q-Q7 mate.

5. P-K7

Anro, 1938
CAPABLANCA

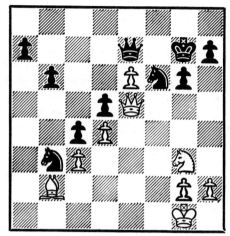

BOTWINNICK
Diagram 88

Nothing can stop this pawn, and so Black must try for a perpetual check of the White King. White's problem is to get his King to a square where he will be safe from further harassment. Botwinnick had seen this before he sacrificed his Bishop and he felt secure in his analysis.

5. . . .	Q-B8 ch.
6. K-B2	Q-B7 ch.
7. K-N3	Q-Q6 ch.
8. K-R4	Q-K5 ch.
9. KxP	Q-K7 ch.
10. K-R4	Q-K5 ch.
11. P-N4	Q-K8 ch.
12. K-R5	Resigns

Black is faced with an imminent checkmate at White's KB8 and he can't stop that and the pawn. If 12. . . . P-R3; 13. Q-B8 ch., K-R2; 14. Q-B7 ch., K-R; 15. P-K8 ch., QxQ; 16. QxQ ch., etc.

White was able to achieve the position he knew he could win with through the sacrifice of two pieces. Once he started the sequence, it could not be stopped without disastrous consequences for White. As we mentioned in the beginning of Chapter III, the number of possible moves in even a short series is astronomical. More important than accurate prediction is an understanding of the principles involved and the development of an intuitive sense that a certain position will be a winning or drawing one. This comes from play and the study of how other contestants have handled similar situations.

Consider the handling of Rooks in middle-game play. By and large, they have not entered the battle in the opening phase, because, like the Queen, they are too valuable to be introduced early, when they would be subjected to indignities from pawns, Knights, and Bishops. But now the Kings have probably been castled, the Rooks are connected, which is their most efficient state, files are being opened up, and minor pieces have left the field. The time is propitious for their entry. Now they can be employed in the seizure and control of open files, rampaging behind enemy lines, battering at fortifications behind which a nervous King waits with trepidation, and supporting their own pawns in their drive to the eighth rank.

Leipzig, 1894
VON SCHEVE

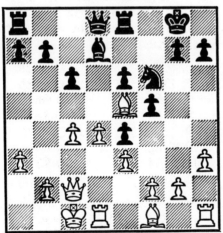

TARRASCH
Diagram 89

In this position, Dr. Tarrasch, a frequent tournament winner in the early part of this century, was handling the White pieces. His strategic plan was to open a major. assault against the enemy's King, spearheaded by his Rooks. The first step involved the opening of the KN file.

1. P-B3!	PxP
2. PxP	P-QN4
3. R-N	R-KB
4. R-Q2!	R-B2

Black sees what is coming and is desperately shoring up his defenses.

5. QR-N2	P-QR4
6. Q-B2	N-K
7. R-N5!	Q-K2
8. Q-R4	

Now Black must guard against Q-R6 and R-R5 by White.

8. . . .	N-B3
9. Q-R6	R-R2
10. B-Q6!!	

This timely move deflects the Black Queen from its most important task, the protection of the King.

10.	QxB
11. RxP ch.	K-B
12. PxP ch.	K-K2
13. RxR ch.	KxR
14. R-N7 ch.	K-K
15. QxN	Resigns

San Sebastian, 1911
NIMZOWITCH

TEICHMANN
Diagram 90

Aron Nimzowitsch was one of the early exponents of the effective use of Rooks in the middle game and this example, taken from a game with Teichmann, Richard the

Third, whom we mentioned in Chapter V, shows how their immense power can be brought to bear, through an open file, on the King's sanctuary.

Black's plan, again, was to crack open the KR file.

1. ...	R-R!
2. N(Q2)-B	P-R4!
3. PxP	RxP
4. B-Q5	QR-R

The first phase of the Black plan has been carried out.

5. BxB	QxB
6. Q-B4	Q-N3!
7. K-N2	N-K3
8. R-K2	

This was essential to prevent 8. ... RxNch.!; 9. NxR, RxNch.; 10. KxR, Q-B7 ch.; 11. K-R3, B-B5; 12. KR-N, N-N4 ch.! etc.

8. ...	N-Q5
9. R(2)-K	Q-N2
10. RxN	PxR
11. N-K4	Q-N3
12. P-B4	B-K2
13. R-Q	P-B4!
14. N-B2	PxP
15. QxP ch.	QxQ
16. RxQ	P-Q4
17. P-N4	B-B4!
18. R-Q	R-R5
19. RxP	BxN
20. KxB	RxP
21. K-K3	R-QB!
22. KxP	R-B5 ch.
23. K-Q3	R(B5)xKBP

Black now has a won ending, with material superiority and a passed pawn, and, in fact, Nimzowitsch did win in another ten moves or so.

Consider for a moment the importance of your pawn structure in the two stages of the game we have discussed up to this point. In the ending, the final decision may hang on the placement of these potential candidates for royalty. In the middle game, having the right kind of pawn formation can be vital in repelling an attack or keeping enemy outposts from becoming established too close to your sphere of influence. Careful handling of your pawns will free your forces for attack and defense and increase their efficiency. Pawns can be used to support Knights and Bishops in advanced positions where they will harass the enemy and spearhead sorties and invasions. To obtain a clear picture of the principles involved in pawn play, we will first examine some of their characteristics without the presence of any other pieces on the board. Diagram 91 shows the White pawns at the beginning of a game. The Black pawns have been placed randomly. The X's show the squares they can capture on—the squares they may be said to control. Clearly the White pawns, arranged as they are in a solid phalanx, effectively bar the way to any invasion force, while none of the dark squares on the Black side of the board is in any way guarded by the Black pawns. Unless Black pieces are relegated to protecting these open avenues into Black territory, an invasion will not have any serious difficulty.

Since it is impossible to develop any pieces except the Knights without moving the pawns, this configuration of the White pawns in Diagram 91 will never be seen in play on a chessboard. But the principle is sound. *The pawns should only be moved for a good reason, and never for want of something better to do. Remember that a pawn, once moved, can never return to that square.*

It is also easy to see from Diagram 92 that doubled pawns, as the two White

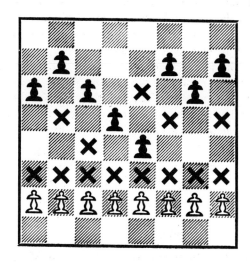

Diagram 91

pawns on QR3 and QR4 are called, are extremely weak; they can never give each other any support and are ready prey for any passing marauders. Consequently, when you have doubled pawns you must reserve some of your forces to defend them, and this means you are left with a smaller mobile force for attack and defense.

Diagram 92

Still referring to this diagram, the Black pawn at KB2 is considered "backward," i.e. it is without the protection of its fellow pawns and, like the isolated Black pawn on QN2, if it is attacked it must be defended by pieces or surrendered. Similarly with the White pawn on KB2. Sometimes backward pawns can be returned to the fold by advancing them, but when this is done other weaknesses are almost invariably created. Let us see how some of these weaknesses can be exploited in a game.

Black has managed to post a Knight in the vulnerable hole in the White pawn formation at Q6. The fact that this Knight is supported by another enables Black to break open the entire Queen side by

1. . . .	NxB
2. RxN	N-Q6
3. R-N	NxNP!
4. RxN	RxN
5. R-N	P-N7
6. Resigns	

Black threatens to play 6. . . . R-R8, and the promotion of the pawn, or its dear

Arnstadt, 1926

NIMZOWITSCH

HAGE

Diagram 93

purchase by the White side, is unavoidable.

One more beautiful example emphasizes the importance of timing in a combination. In this game, played between Capablanca and Subarev in Moscow in 1925, White has a marked advantage in space while material is equal. Black's forces seem to be defending adequately with doubled Rooks in the center, the Queen and the Rook protecting the NP (which is attacked by White's Queen and Rook). White has an isolated pawn in an advanced position that he can protect only with pieces. White's Knight is well posted, bearing as it does on the center, but Black threatens to take it off with his Bishop and break up White's King-side pawns.

If White has any plans to convert his spatial advantages into material superiority, now is the time. (In chess, as in life, lost opportunities rarely become available a second time.) White strikes with

    1. RxR ch.   KxR

Black's move is forced. If the Queen or the Rook recapture, White pushes his pawn to Q6, discovering a check to the Black King and then capturing the piece on K7 with the pawn.

    2. QxP

CAPABLANCA

Diagram 94

Now if Black exchanges Queens, the White Rook raises havoc on the seventh rank with the Black pawns and wins the end game in short order. Black also has to guard against 3. R-K ch., K-Q3; 4. Q-N6 ch.! But Black needs to exchange some of White's attacking pieces and get them out of the action as quickly as possible.

2. . . .	BxN!
3. R-K ch.!	B-K4
4. P-Q6 ch.!!	

Now what? The Black pieces cannot take the pawn, since they are both pinned to the King. If the King takes it, the White Rook checks him at Q and wins the Queen. The King must move, while still protecting his Queen, which is under attack from the heavy guns of the White Queen. If he goes to his Queen square, the check by the White Queen at N6 forces him to the B square where another check by the White Rook is disastrous. Hence, all he can do is

| 4. . . . | K-K3 |
| 5. Q-N3 ch. | K-B4 |

This is the beginning of the end. The King has been forced away from the protection of his major defenders and into White's home territory.

| 6. Q-Q3 ch. | K-N4 |

Why not back again with K-K3? Because then the next White check is at QB4 and when the King is forced back to B4, Q-KN4 is checkmate!

| 7. Q-K3 ch. | K-B4 |

If K-R4, 8.P-N4 ch., K-R5; 9. Q-N3 mate!

8. Q-K4 ch.!	K-K3
9. Q-B4 ch.	KxP
10. R-Q ch.	

Winning the Queen and, not long after, the game.

All of these sample games were picked to show the tremendous vibrancy of the middle game. The combinations are all there, waiting to be put in action, to be discharged with an explosive force that reaches beyond the chessboard and into the minds of the players.

9.

THE
OPENING

THE OPENING

WHEN THE SUN ROSE that brisk October morning in 1415, its rays sparkled on the gleaming armor of five thousand Frenchmen of noble birth gathered in a little field near Agincourt. In full panoply they waited, barring the way of the invader. Indifferent to strategy and the niceties of preparation, the Grand Seneschal of France allowed his forces to form three rough lines—each a deep mass—with the cavalry in front, men-at-arms and archers in the rear.

Across the mud-soaked field, the smaller English army waited silently. King Henry and his knight generals had paid careful attention to preparation and the skillful deployment of their units. Behind a palisade of pikes and spears, he had positioned his crossbowmen and the archers with their famous English yew long bows. His armored cavalry and foot soldiers protected their rear and flanks.

The French viewed these maneuvers with disdain; leather-clad archers standing up to steel-encased lancers and mace wielders? Insulting. They charged.

Military analysts agree that history might have taken a different tack if the French had not launched this premature assault with their most valuable units—their heavily armored, mounted knights. Quickly bogged down in the mud, trapped by *chevaux de frise,*° they were cut to shreds by the illiterate spear-thrusting, ax-swinging English peasants.

When Henry took time from his kingly duties and sat down for a little relaxation at the chessboard, he must have felt right at home. No launcher of the premature attack he, no ignorer of the importance of wise development—he had learned his lessons well in a different school.

Sitting down in front of the chessboard, with the pieces set up (as in Diagram 1 on page 12) and the game about to begin, you are in a situation similar, in many ways, to that of King Henry and Grand Seneschal d'Albret, Constable of France, before the Battle of Agincourt. You know your own forces and you know your opponent's. You know the battlefield and the objective, and

°Timber covered with iron-pointed spikes and spears used as a defense against calvary.

you have a basic, preliminary strategy in mind that you are going to try and execute. What you do not know is what is in your opponent's mind, what his strategy is. And this will not be revealed until the preliminary, developing moves have been made and the issue is about to be joined. The feints and probes, the sorties and thrusts to find weaknesses, all help to reveal his plan. Your opening moves must place your pieces where they will have maximum offensive and defensive capability and where they will work together well in smooth coordination.

Because White has the first move, White has the initiative, and this is a slight advantage. If you are playing White, you must try to use this to secure a better position first, and then, when your troops are marshaled in the staging area, launch your attack. If you are in charge of the Black pieces, your problem is different; you must strive to obtain equality, to develop your pen for defense first, and then, when you've parried your opponent's assault, to launch a counterattack of your own.

The two fundamental concepts that dominate the opening are development of the pieces and control of the center squares shown in Diagram 43. Chess theories and studious analysis are constantly being tested in pragmatic, over-the-board play in tournaments and matches between the strongest players in the world—the masters and Grand Masters who are the professionals of the game. The guidelines we can deduce from this exhaustive research are several:

1. It is generally best to open with P-K4, P-Q4, or P-QB4. These moves exert immediate pressure on the center and open lines for further development.

2. The minor pieces (Knights first and then Bishops) should be quickly placed in good squares where they will also have effect on the center, and they should not be moved more than once until the other pieces are developed *unless there is a compelling reason.*

3. When it is possible to make a developing move and a threatening move at the same time, do so. This slows down your opponent's development and forces him to shift to meet your threat.

4. The Queen and Rooks should not be brought out too early in the game (remember Agincourt!) since their harassment will force you to waste moves and lose tempo.

5. Keep your pawn moves to a minimum and make every effort to avoid a weakened pawn structure.

6. Plan on Castling your King early and before your opponent can get an attack started. Kingside Castling usually is slightly preferable.

7. Always play to get and keep control of the center. This can be done by maintaining strong center pawns, or by having your pieces bear on the center, or by having them occupy the center, or by a combination of all three.

8. Avoid premature attacks and sacrifices *unless a positive advantage can be realized.*

As we play out some of the games in this section, apply these principles and see them in operation. Above all, measure your every move in the opening against these tests; how does your contemplated move affect the center? And how does it bear on the development of your other pieces? When your opponent moves, ask yourself what he threatens and what his reason was for making that move. Be prepared to change your strategic plans at a moment's notice if necessary to meet a new threat, seize a new initiative, or win an advantage. But maintain your guard against an offer of golden apples by your adversary that will in reality deflect you from your objective or lure your forces into ambush.

Now, let us consider some major openings° and see how other players have met these challenges. One of the oldest known openings, the Ruy Lopez, was systematically studied by a Spanish priest of that name in the sixteenth century. It has probably been played more than any other P-K4 sequence, since it effectively challenges Black for control of the center.

To understand the general pattern of moves of the Ruy Lopez, let us consider each move individually—its purpose, objective, and effect. With

1. P-K4

White moves to control the center and open up the KB diagonal.

1. . . .　　　　　　　　　　　P-K4

Black has the same objective.

2. N-KB3

This develops the Knight to an ideal square, attacking the Black pawn on K4 and exerting additional thrust on the important center.

2. . . .　　　　　　　　　　　N-QB3

Thus developing, defending the pawn, and meeting the challenge.

3. B-N5

This is the characteristic move that identifies the Ruy Lopez. By threatening to remove the defender, the pawn on K4 is further jeopardized.

3. . . .　　　　　　　　　　　P-QR3

This strategically important move has a hidden barb. If 4. BxN, QPxB; 5. NxP, Q-Q5! and Black gets back his pawn, ends up with two Bishops, and may prevent White from Castling (by exchanging Queens on White's K2).

4. B-R4

Retaining the option to exchange so that

°General patterns of opening moves have names such as The King's Gambit, The Queen's Gambit, The French Defense, The Sicilian Defense, etc. The main lines and variations are analyzed in detail in *Modern Chess Openings* by Horowitz and *The Ideas Behind the Chess Openings* by Fine.

when the White KP is protected, the threat to remove the Black Knight becomes real.

4. . . .　　　　　　　　　　　N-B3

Thus developing, attacking, and pressuring the center.

5. 0-0

The King is removed to a safe haven, developing the Rook and, indirectly, defending the P on K4. If Black takes it with the Knight, White's R-K or P-Q4 wins it back and subjects Black to a possible pin of his Knight to his King. Black must not allow his King to remain uncastled much longer.

5. . . .　　　　　　　　　　　B-K2

Developing and protecting the King and preparing for a King-side castle.

6. R-K

Protecting the pawn, bringing the Rook to bear on important squares, *and reactivating the threat to remove the Black Knight on QB3 with BxN, followed by the capture of the Black pawn on K4. Now Black must prevent this.*

6. . . .　　　　　　　　　　　P-QN4

This ends the BxN menace and keeps up with White in the center.

7. B-N3

This is the only move to save the Bishop.

7. . . .　　　　　　　　　　　P-Q3

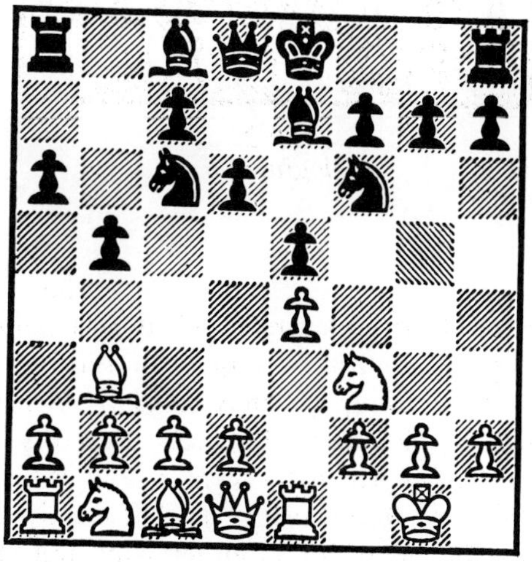

Diagram 95

This provides additional protection for the KP and opens another route for the QB. Black is about even with White in this position.

Over-the-board play, does, of course, vary from the theoretical. Chess players are, above all else, innovative and imaginative and constantly testing new lines. One of the greatest of modern players, Paul Keres, was pitted against the many-times German champion, Wolfgang Unzicker:

RUY LOPEZ

White: Keres	Black: Unzicker
1. P-K4	P-K4
2. N-KB3	N-QB3
3. B-N5	N-B3
4. 0-0	NxP
5. P-Q4	B-K2
6. Q-K2	N-Q3
7. BxN	NPxB
8. PxP	N-N2

UNZICKER

KERES

Diagram 96

How do the players stand at this point? White has control over more of the board, the White King is safely castled, White's Knight, which is well placed, supports an important pawn in the center, and White's Queen is strategically placed, ready to throw her influence to either wing but still out of reach of Black threats.

Black, on the other hand, still has his King in the middle of the board, he has used up four of his eight moves on his King Knight, and it is located in a poor square with no influence on the center. In effect, Black has totally abdicated his struggle for the center. As a small compensation, Black does have a pair of Bishops that may be dangerous in the middle and end games.

Let's see how the game proceeded from here.

9. N-B3	0-0
10. N-Q4	B-B4
11. R-Q	BxN
12. RxB	P-Q4
13. PxP e.p.	PxP

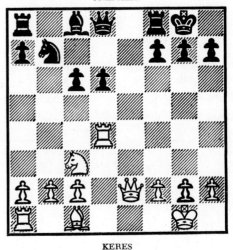

UNZICKER

KERES

Diagram 97

Black now has his King safely castled, but he still only has one piece, the Knight, developed, and not in a good position at that. He has given up one of his valuable Bishops and only has minimal influence in the vital center. White, on the other hand, has three pieces well developed and will shortly commence a serious assault against the Black King's stronghold. Black never recovers from these disadvantages in the opening, and loses in another fourteen or so moves.

The following Ruy Lopez has Black seizing a commanding open Queen file and exerting tremendous pressure on an uncastled White Kings.

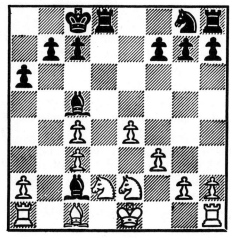

WERLINSKI

ALEKHINE

Diagram 98

RUY LOPEZ

White: Werlinski   *Black*: Alekhine

1.	P-K4	P-K4
2.	N-KB3	N-QB3
3.	B-N5	P-QR3
4.	BxN	QPxB
5.	P-Q4	PxP
6.	QxP	QxQ
7.	NxQ	P-QB4
8.	N-K2	B-Q2
9.	P-QN3	P-B5
10.	PxP	B-R5
11.	P-QB3?	0-0-0
12.	N-Q2	B-B7
13.	P-B3	B-B4!

White has material superiority in the extra pawn, but this is one of those golden apples we referred to earlier. Black deliberately sacrificed that pawn on the ninth move to achieve this position. Black's two Bishops and Rook dominate the board, holding White's King in the center (the Bishop on B4 prevents White from castling) where he will be subjected to all sorts of indignities from the lower-class citizenry. When Black's Knight comes out and the King Rook moves to the King square, Black will be completely and effectively developed. White has a long way to go, since, without castling, it will be costly and tedious to get the King Rook into the game.

The White Knights are poorly placed, but cannot move readily (moving the Knight on Q2 leads to instant mate when the Black Rook comes to Q8) and the Queen Bishop is blocked. White never was able to castle and resigned a few moves later.

The King's Gambit,[*] a favorite of Morphy and Marshall, two of the greatest of American players, is not seen much in important tournaments today, but it is very popular in chess clubs and coffee houses all over the world. It should definitely be in your repertoire. The central theme of this opening is the early surrender of a pawn for an edge in development and position. Very precise play by Black is essential for survival when White's attack reaches full crest. Again, we shall take it up, move by move.

1. P-K4

White moves to control the center and open up the KB diagonal.

1. . . .   P-K4

Black has the same objective.

2. P-KB4!

The gambit pawn. It attacks Black's KP and forces an immediate decision.

2. . . .   PxP

The gauntlet has been thrown and taken. White is not planning on recovering this pawn for some time, but will concentrate on preparing for an attack directly against the Black King and his weakest square— KB2.

3. N-KB3

Thus developing the Knight to its ideal square and preventing the Black Queen from disrupting plans with a check at R5.

3. . . .   P-KN4

The purpose here is to protect the pawn as quickly as possible and to try to hamper the White attack by preventing a buildup of pieces.

[*]We are also indebted to the Spanish priest-scholar Ruy Lopez for his introduction of "gambit" into chess terminology, meaning a sacrifice of some material, usually a pawn, for some positional advantage in the opening.

4. P-KR4

The effect is to attack the base of the pawn chain and force Black to find other defensive resources. The Black Knight pawn cannot be supported by P-R3 because of PxP, and if the P on R3 recaptures, White wins with RxR!

4. . . .   P-N5!

This adds a little sand to the White Machinery.

5. N-K5

This gets the Knight away from the sting of the pawn *and launches an attack at the Black King side—particularly, Black's KB2.*

5. . . .   N-KB3

Developing, protecting, and attacking.

6. P-Q4

Not P-Q3, which would block the White King Bishop. This move strikes at the center, and exposes the Black BP to attack from the White Queen Bishop.

6. . . .   P-Q3

Adding a defender to the Black NP and driving the White N.

7. N-Q3

Another piece on the Black KBP.

7. . . .   NxP!

Diagram 99

Breaking up White's strong pawn phalanx in the center and conceding the BP in exchange.

How do the positions compare at this juncture? White has moved his Knight three times, but Black has used up several moves with his pawns. Black has somewhat more control of the board and is two pawns ahead. White will shortly capture the KB pawn and develop another piece. The King-side pawn structures are broken up and King-side castling is unattractive for both sides. The center is still in a state of flux—with neither side having any significant advantage. On balance, Black would seem to have a very slight superior position. The game might proceed as follows:

8. BxP   Q-K2

Threatening a discovered check, which is met with

9. Q-K2   B-N2

Developing, threatening the QP, and bearing on the center.

10. P-B3   P-KR4

Before White can prevent this with P-R5. Now the Black NP is secure.

11. N-Q2   NxN
12. KxN!

White's advantage in development is becoming more noticeable.

12. . . .   QxQ
13. BxQ

And now White has an easily discernible edge in development; not only are all his minor pieces out, but they are in relevant squares (although the KB could be better placed) *and his Rooks are connected.* Black, on the other hand, will have some problems bringing his Rooks into play.

13. . . .   B-B4
14. KR-KB

Seizing an important open file and anticipating QR-Q or K!

14. . . .   N-Q2?

Not the best place for the Knight. B3 is better.

15. N-N4

Now threatening to win a pawn with 16. BxP, PxB; 17. RxB. This was not available while the Knight was still at Q3 because if BxP, BxN!

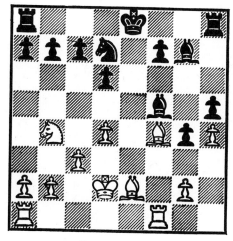

Diagram 100

15. . . .	N-B3
16. B-N5 ch.	B-Q2?
17. QR-K ch.	K-Q
18. B-N5!	BxB
19. RxN! Resigns	

After 19. . . . BxR; White wins with 20. BxB ch., K-Q2; 21. R-K7 ch., K-Q; 22. R-K5 dis. ch. and 23. RxB or if 21. . . . K-B; 22. BxR, etc.

Strictly speaking, we went past the opening, but the able way White converted his better development into a win is relevant to much that was discussed in the chapters on *Strategy and Tactics* (V.), *The Stages of a Chess Game* (VI.), and *The Middle Game* (VIII.).

Can White determine on the opening and force Black to play his game? If White moves 1. P-K4, is Black forced into a particular opening he may detest or be weak in? No. There are a variety of defensive openings at Black's disposal such as the Sicilian Defense, the French Defense, the Petroff Defense, and the Caro-Kann Defense that prevent White from having an arbitrary choice. There are also many responses to 1. P-Q4, and each of these, in turn, has many variations. Familiarity with two or three basic openings and defenses *and an understanding of the principles behind the openings* will make you a chess player who cannot be taken lightly. Some of the books listed in the appendix will be helpful.

And just as every good general studies the military campaigns of wars long since fought and won (or lost), so you should play over the games of the masters—the current games reported in newspapers and chess periodicals and the classics from tournaments and matches. Such a selection will be found in the next chapter.

A last word. Nothing is as good as playing. Join a club or find that mysterious graveyard of the elephants that exists in every city, town, and village where chess players of all shapes, sizes, strengths, and ages (and, recently, sex) congregate. Sometimes it is a coffee house, sometimes a bookstore after hours, sometimes a library or parish house. It is out there waiting to be found, and found with it will be some of the best friends you will make in life.

10.
SELECTED
GAMES

THESE GAMES HAVE BEEN CHOSEN for several reasons. They are exciting, they show how ten or so different openings might be played, and they are instructive examples that demonstrate the practical methods of using some of the principles we have covered. They are all from master play, but are arranged in an order of increasing complexity. My suggestion is that you examine each move and search for its rationale. Then pause at each diagram and consider what the next moves might be. At the end of each game give some thought as to why one side or the other resigned at that point and search for the continuation that the winning side might have followed to seal the victory.

RUY LOPEZ

White: Khodko   Black: Zaslavsky

	White	Black
1.	P-K4	P-K4
2.	N-KB3	N-QB3
3.	B-N5	P-QR3
4.	B-R4	P-QN4
5.	B-N3	N-R4
6.	0-0	NxB
7.	RPxN	P-Q3
8.	P-Q4	B-N2
9.	N-B3	N-B3
10.	Q-K2	PxP
11.	NxQP	B-K2
12.	R-Q	P-N5
13.	P-K5!	N-Q2
14.	PxP	PxP

ZASLAVSKY

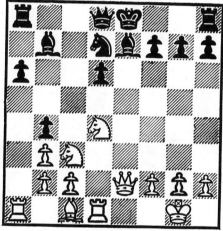

KHODKO

Diagram 101

	White	Black
15.	N-B5!	PxN
16.	NxNP ch.	K-B
17.	B-R6	K-N
18.	N-K6!	B-B6!
19.	PxB	Q-QB
20.	K-R	P-B3
21.	N-Q8!!	Resigns

White threatens mate in two ways: 22. R-N mate (since the Knight blocks escape at B7) and, if 21. . . . QxN; 22. Q-K6 mate!

93

	White: Cheremisin	Black: Artiushikhin
1.	P-K4	P-K4
2.	P-KB4	PxP
3.	N-KB3	N-KB3
4.	P-K5	N-R4
5.	P-KN4!!	PxP e.p.
6.	P-Q4	P-Q4
7.	N-N5	P-KN3
8.	PxP	B-K2
9.	RxN!	PxR
10.	QxP	BxN
11.	BxB	Q-Q2
12.	N-B3	P-QB3
13.	Q-R6	Q-K3
14.	Q-N7!	R-B
15.	B-Q3	P-KB4
16.	B-K2!	N-Q2
17.	B-R5 ch.	R-B2
18.	N-K2!	N-B
19.	N-B4	Q-Q2

ARTIUSHIKHIN

CHEREMISIN

Diagram 102

20.	Q-N8!	Resigns

Threatening 21. P-K6 and 21. B-R6. While both Kings remained uncastled in this game, Black's problems with development made his King's exposure fatal.

SICILIAN DEFENSE

White: Bykhovsky   Black: Antoshin

1.	P-K4	P-QB4
2.	P-QB4?	N-QB3
3.	N-QB3	P-K3
4.	P-KN3	N-B3
5.	B-N2	P-Q4!
6.	KPxP	PxP
7.	NxP	NxN
8.	PxN	N-N5
9.	P-QR3?	N-Q6 ch.!
10.	K-B	B-K2
11.	B-K4?	0-0!
12.	K-N2	P-B5
13.	N-K2	B-R6! ch.
14.	K-N	B-N4
15.	N-B3	P-B4
16.	BxN	PxB
17.	P-QN4	B-B3
18.	Q-B3	R-K
19.	B-N2	Q-K2
20.	Q-K3	B-Q5
21.	QxQ	RxQ
22.	P-Q6	R-K3
23.	N-R4	QR-K
24.	R-KB	. . .

ANTOSHIN

BYKHOVSKY

Diagram 103

24.	. . .	R-K8
	Resigns	

There is no way to prevent mate either at
K8 or B8.

95

FRENCH DEFENSE

FRENCH DEFENSE

White: Winawer	*Black*: DeVere
1. P-K4	
1. P-K4	P-K3
2. P-Q4	P-Q4
3. N-QB3	B-N5
4. B-Q3	PxP
5. BxP	P-QB4
6. N-K2	PxP
7. NxP	BxN ch.
8. PxB	Q-R4
9. Q-B3	N-KB3
10. BxNP	BxB
11. QxB	QxP ch.
12. K-K2	QxN
13. QxR	0-0
14. R-QN	Q-B5 ch.
15. K-K	N-B3
16. Q-N7	N-Q5
Resigns	

DE VERE

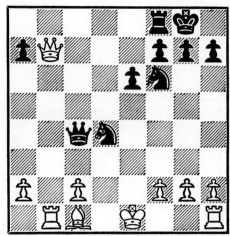

WINAWER

Diagram 104

The mate that is looming up at K2 cannot be stopped by the White Queen because the Black Knights cover all the important squares (N5, K4, and B3). If the White tries to escape via Q2, a wild chase develops, starting with 17. . . . QxP ch., forcing the King into the center of the board and disaster. Work out this skirmish.

White: Burn   *Black*: DeVere

1. P-K4	P-K3
2. P-Q4	P-Q4
3. PxP	PxP
4. B-Q3	B-Q3
5. N-KB3	N-QB3
6. 0-0	N-B3
7. R-K ch.	B-K3
8. B-B5	0-0!
9. BxB	PxB
10. RxP	N-K5
11. P-B4	. . .

DE VERE

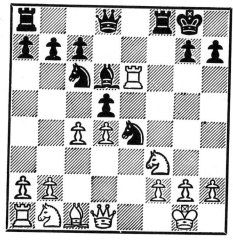

BURN

Diagram 105

11. . . .	RxN!!
12. PxR	Q-R5
13. RxB	QxBP ch.
14. K-R	NxR
15. PxP	R-K
16. B-Q2	R-K7
Resigns	

Black threatens mate at N7 and R7 and 17. Q-N, which prevents these, is powerless against 17. . . . QxBP ch.

97

White: Naegeli   Black: Euwe

	White	Black
1.	P-K4	N-KB3
2.	P-K5	N-Q4
3.	P-Q4	P-Q3
4.	P-QB4	N-N3
5.	P-B4	B-B4
6.	N-KB3	PxP
7.	BPxP	P-K3
8.	N-B3	N-B3
9.	B-K3	Q-Q2
10.	B-K2	0-0-0
11.	Q-Q2	P-B3
12.	PxP	PxP
13.	0-0	R-N
14.	KR-Q	Q-N2
15.	B-B	N-K4!
16.	NxN	PxN
17.	Q-KB2	B-KN5
18.	R-Q2	PxP
19.	BxP?	RxB
20.	RxR	B-QB4
21.	R-Q8 ch.	RxR
22.	QxB	R-Q7
23.	N-K4	RxQNP
24.	N-Q6 ch.	K-Q2
25.	N-N5	K-B
26.	R-K	K-N
27.	R-K5	B-B4
28.	Q-Q4	. . .

	White	Black
30.	K-B2	Q-B3
31.	B-K2	B-K5 dis. ch.
	Resigns	

In addition to having a poor end game, White now loses the exchange.

EUWE

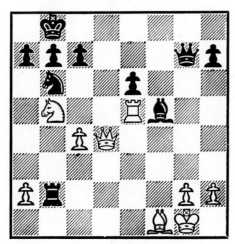

NAEGELI

Diagram 106

28.	. . .	R-Q7!
29.	Q-K3	R-Q

PETROFF DEFENSE

White: Spielmann   *Black*: Marshall

	White	Black
1.	P-K4	P-K4
2.	N-KB3	N-KB3
3.	NxP	P-Q3
4.	N-KB3	NxP
5.	P-Q4	P-Q4
6.	B-Q3	B-Q3
7.	0-0	B-KN5
8.	P-B4	0-0!
9.	PxP	P-KB4
10.	N-B3	N-Q2!
11.	P-KR3	B-R4
12.	NxN	PxN
13.	BxP	N-B3
14.	B-B5	K-R
15.	P-KN4	NxQP
16.	Q-Q3	N-N5
17.	Q-K4	B-B2
18.	B-N5	Q-K
19.	N-K5	B-Q4
20.	Q-K2	N-B3
21.	Q-Q3	NxN
22.	PxN	QxP
23.	Q-KN3	QxP!
24.	Q-R4	RxB!
25.	PxR	Q-K4
26.	Q-N3	QxP
27.	Q-N4	Q-K4
28.	KR-K	Q-R7 ch.
29.	K-B	R-KB
30.	K-K2	QxP ch.
31.	K-Q3	P-N4!
	Resigns	

MARSHALL

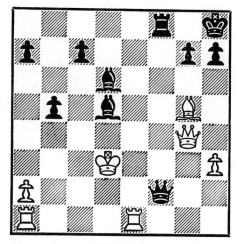

SPIELMANN

Diagram 107

The denuded White King is about to be racked by the Bishops, starting with 32. ... B-B5 ch., and there is no escape haven; Black will either mate or win substantial material. For example, if 32. QR-QB, R-B6 ch.; 33. R-K3, B-B5 ch.; 34. RxB, PxR ch.; 35. KxP, RxR, etc. or 32. KR-QB, R-B6 ch. or 32. B-Q2, B-B5 ch.; 33. K-B2, B-N5; 34. KR-Q, R-Q; 35. Q-N5, R-Q4; 36. Q-B4, RxB ch.; 37. RxR, QxQ; 38. R-Q8 ch., B-N etc.

CARO-KANN DEFENSE

White: Jevsejev   *Black*: Flohr

1.	P-K4	P-QB3
2.	P-Q4	P-Q4
3.	N-QB3	PxP
4.	NxP	N-Q2
5.	N-KB3	KN-B3
6.	N-N3	P-K3
7.	B-Q3	B-K2
8.	0-0	0-0
9.	Q-K2	P-B4
10.	P-B3	P-QN3
11.	N-K5	B-N2
12.	P-KB4	PxP
13.	PxP	NxN
14.	QPxN	N-N5!
15.	BxP ch.	KxB
16.	QxN	Q-Q5 ch.
17.	K-R	QR-B
18.	N-R5	P-N3
19.	Q-R3	R-KR
20.	N-B6 ch.	K-N2
21.	Q-K3	. . .

FLOHR

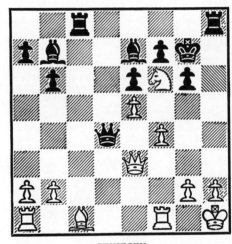

JEVSEJEV

Diagram 108

21.	. . .	R-B7!
22.	Q-KN3	Q-Q6!
23.	QxQ	RxKNP
24.	N-N4	R(7) x RP ch.!!
	Resigns	

White had been hoping for 24. . . . RxN dis. ch. (from the Bishop), when 25. R-B3 might give White some further play, but Black's move in the game leads to a speedy mate: 25. K-N, R-N7 mate.

White: Miroshnichenko   Black: Anokhin

1.	P-Q4	N-KB3
2.	P-QB4	P-K3
3.	N-QB3	P-Q4
4.	N-B3	P-B4
5.	BPxP	KPxP
6.	B-N5	B-K3
7.	P-K3	B-K2
8.	B-N5 ch.	KN-Q2
9.	BxB	QxB
10.	PxP	QxP
11.	0-0	0-0
12.	R-B	N-QB3
13.	BxN	QxB
14.	N-Q4	Q-Q3
15.	QN-N5	Q-K4
16.	Q-N3!	N-N3
17.	P-B4	Q-B3
18.	N-B7	QR-Q
19.	Q-R3	P-QR3
20.	P-B5	B-B

ANOKHIN

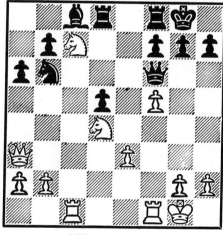

MIROSHNICHENKO

Diagram 109

21.	N(Q4)-K6!	N-B5
22.	NxQP!	Q-K4
23.	N-K7 ch.	K-R
24.	NxQR!	NxQ
25.	NxP ch.	Resigns

After 25. . . . RxN; White has 26. RxB ch., etc.

QUEEN'S GAMBIT DECLINED

White: Alekhine	Black: Euwe
1. P-Q4	P-Q4
2. N-KB3	P-QB4
3. P-B4	P-K3
4. P-K3	N-QB3
5. N-B3	N-B3
6. P-QR3	B-Q3
7. PxBP	BxBP
8. P-QN4	B-Q3
9. B-N2	0-0
10. R-B	Q-K2!
11. PxP	PxP
12. NxP	NxN
13. QxN	P-QR4!
14. B-N5	PxP
15. P-QR4	R-Q?
16. Q-R5	P-N3
17. Q-R6	N-K4

EUWE

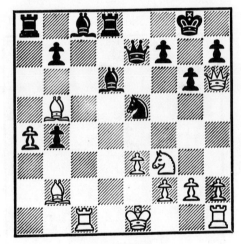

ALEKHINE

Diagram 110

18. N-N5	P-B3
19. BxN	PxB
20. B-B4 ch.	Resigns

Look at the possibilities here. If 20. . . .
K-R; 21. N-B7 ch., K-N; 22. NxR dis. ch.,
K-R; 23. N-B7 ch., K-N; 24. NxB dis. ch.
and Black is wasted!

White: Capablanca   *Black*: Nimzowitsch

1. P-Q4	N-KB3
2. P-QB4	P-K3
3. N-QB3	B-N5
4. Q-B2	P-Q4
5. B-N5	PxP
6. N-B3	P-N4
7. P-QR4	P-B3
8. BxN	PxB
9. P-KN3	P-QR3
10. B-N2	R-R2
11. O-O	R-Q2
12. Q-B	O-O
13. Q-R6	BxN
14. PxB	K-R
15. N-Q2	P-KB4
16. KR-N	P-K4
17. N-B3	R-Q3
18. Q-K3	P-K5
19. N-Q2	N-Q2
20. P-N4	N-B3
21. NPxP	BxP
22. Q-B4	Q-Q2
23. BxP	NxB
24. NxN	R-N3 ch.
25. N-N3	BxR
26. RxB	P-KB4
27. P-B3	Q-KN2
28. K-B2	Q-B3
29. PxP	BPxP
30. R-Q	K-N
31. P-Q5!	QxP
32. P-Q6	Q-B3

33. P-Q7	P-B6
34. NxP!	P-B7!
35. R-Q6!	Q-Q
36. Q-K5!!	RxN
37. Q-K8 ch.!	R-B

NIMZOWITSCH

CAPABLANCA

Diagram 111

38. RxR ch.	Drawn

After 38. ... PxR; 39. QxP ch., K-R; 40. Q-R6 ch., White has a perpetual check. This is a fine example of how White managed to use his Queen pawn to force a draw in a really desperate situation.

ENGLISH OPENING

White: Zukertort   *Black*: Blackburne

1.	P-QB4	P-K3
2.	P-K3	N-KB3
3.	N-KB3	P-QN3
4.	B-K2	B-N2
5.	0-0	P-Q4
6.	P-Q4	B-Q3
7.	N-B3	0-0
8.	P-QN3	QN-Q2
9.	B-N2	Q-K2
10.	N-QN5	N-K5
11.	NxB	PxN
12.	N-Q2	N(2)-B3
13.	P-B3	NxN
14.	QxN	PxP
15.	BxP	P-Q4
16.	B-Q3	KR-B
17.	QR-K	R-B2
18.	P-K4	QR-QB
19.	P-K5	N-K
20.	P-B4	P-N3
21.	R-K3!	P-B4
22.	PxP e.p.	NxP
23.	P-B5!	N-K5
24.	BxN	PxB
25.	PxNP	R-B7
26.	PxP ch.	K-R
27.	P-Q5 ch.	P-K4

BLACKBURNE

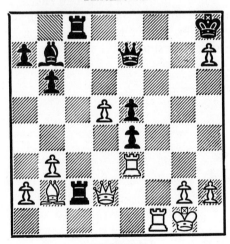

ZUKERTORT

Diagram 112

28.	Q-N4!!	R(1)-B4

If 28. ... QxQ; 29. BxP ch., KxP; and mate follows shortly with 30, R-R3 ch., K-

N3; 31. R-N3 ch., K-R4; 32. R-B5 ch., K-R3; 33. B-B4 ch., K-R2; 34. R-R5 mate.

29.	R-B8 ch.!!	KxP

If 29. ... QxR; 30. BxP ch., KxP; 31. QxP ch., K-R3; 32. R-R3 ch., K-N4, 33. R-N3 ch., K-R4; 34. Q-N4 ch., K-R3; 35. Q-N6 or R3 mate.

30.	QxP ch.	K-N2
31.	BxP ch.	KxR
32.	B-N7 ch.!	K-N
33.	QxQ	Resigns

If 33. ... R-B2; 34. Q-B8 ch., K-R2; 35. R-R3 ch., K-N3; 36. R-N3 ch., K-R2; 37. Q-R8 mate.

PETROFF DEFENSE

White: Lupi   *Black*: Alekhine

1. P-K4	P-K4
2. N-KB3	N-KB3
3. N-B3	B-N5
4. NxP	0-0
5. P-Q3	P-Q4!
6. P-QR3	BxN ch.
7. PxB	R-K
8. P-KB4	PxP
9. P-Q4	N-Q4!
10. P-B4	N-K2
11. B-K2	N-B4
12. P-B3	Q-R5 ch.
13. K-B	P-K6
14. Q-K	QxP ch.
15. K-N	NxP!
16. PxN	QxP
17. R-N	QxN
18. B-N2	Q-KB4
19. R-Q	N-B3
20. R-Q5	Q-B7
21. B-R	B-B4
22. B-Q	Q-N8!
23. Resigns	

ALEKHINE

LUPI

Diagram 113

This is a fascinating and complex position. Black threatens an eventual P-K7, but if executed prematurely the advantage may fade. Work out the different defenses, starting with 23. Q-K2, or 23. B-QB3, and plan Black's attacks.

APPENDIX

Chess tournaments are becoming more and more popular with millions of players competing in thousands of these contests every year. To establish some uniformity, the FIDE and the U.S. Chess Federation have promulgated the following U.S.C.F. Tournament Rules.

USCF TOURNAMENT RULES
With Amendments up to April 1973

The following rules supersede all previously published USCF Tournament Rules.

Tournament Arrangements

1. The organization sponsoring a tournament must be a USCF affiliate and may appoint a local committee to take charge of the arrangements.

2. All games must be played in the tournament rooms on the days and at the times specified by the tournament organizers unless the director makes or accepts other arrangements.

3. The competition must be supervised by a USCF Certified Tournament Director (local, intermediate, or national as required by the type of tournament), who may appoint assistant directors to aid him in the performance of his duties. The director of a tournament above the local level should not play in the tournament.

4. In these rules, "the director" means the director himself. The indefinite, "a director," may mean the director or an assistant director. The term "referee" means a director or any person appointed by the director to supervise play in a game or games. The term "official" may refer to a director, a member of the local committee, or any person appointed to perform duties in connection with the conduct of the tournament.

5. For the inclusive dates of play, every player in the tournament must be a USCF member in good standing, and, in a team tournament, either the sponsoring league must be a USCF affiliate or every team must represent a USCF affiliate.

6. In a Swiss System tournament, the director may, at his discretion, accept entries after the announced closing time, but a late entrant defaults any round he has missed for which it is inconvenient or too late for the director to pair the entrant for play. A bye must not be given simply because a player enters late.

Rating Regulations

7. All played games in a USCF-rated tournament are rated for both players, including games won by time forfeit, games won by failure to appear after adjournment, and games played by a player who subsequently withdrew or was not permitted to continue. Games in which the opponent made no move are considered as unplayed and are not rated.

The duration of the first time-control period must be at least one hour for each player, and the time limit of any control period must not be faster than an average of two minutes per move (thirty moves per hour) in a national tournament, or one and one-half minutes per move (forty moves per hour) in a local or intermediate tournament, except when a time penalty has been imposed under USCF Tournament Rule No. 34d. The USCF Policy Board may make exceptions so that some national tournaments may be played at the faster rate allowed local and intermediate tournaments. If a faster time limit than an average of two minutes per move is used in any tournament, it must be announced in advance.

General Tournament Regulations

8. Play shall be governed by the Laws of the *Fédération Internationale des Échecs* (FIDE) and by the FIDE and USCF interpretations of these laws.

9. In general, the methods of pairing, color allocation, scoring, and tie-breaking in round robin and Swiss System tournaments should follow the recommendations in the *Official Chess Handbook* by Kenneth Harkness (New York: David McKay, c. 1967), approved by the USCF.

10. The following exceptions to normal procedure apply only to large tournaments in which it is impossible to supervise play in all games.

    a. Infringements of the Laws on recording of games (FIDE Article 13, and USCF Tournament Rule Nos. 24–26 herein) and the touched man (FIDE Articles 8 and 20) must be claimed by the opponent unless a director or referee witnesses a violation.

    b. The players are responsible for checking their clocks to see that they are operating properly and must report defects to the director.

    c. If a player wishes to adjust men on their squares when his opponent is absent and an official is not available, he may ask a spectator or a player who is not on the move to witness the adjustment.

    d. In general, it is not always possible to enforce rules or interpretations that depend on constant supervision of a game, but if a director or referee witnesses a violation of

106

any law, rule, or interpretation, it is his duty to require compliance and to warn or penalize the guilty player.

11. As stated in FIDE Articles 8 and 20, it is only the player whose turn it is to move who may adjust men on their squares. If the other player adjusts his own or his opponent's men, he may be penalized at the director's discretion.

Playing Sessions

12. With the exception of any games postponed by consent of the director, all the games of each round must start promptly at the time specified (See USCF Tournament Rule No. 2). If feasible, the director should give five minutes warning, then announce that play must begin.

   In a large tournament, if it is impractical for the director to announce the beginning of a round, players should be urged, in advance, to begin their games promptly by starting their opponents' clocks. The players should also be informed that no permission is needed to start games at the specified time if the pairings have been posted.

13. During playing sessions, players with games in progress should not leave the playing room for extended periods without first informing the director.

   A player who does not wish to continue a lost game and leaves without being courteous enough to resign or notify the director may be severely penalized, at the director's discretion, for poor sportsmanship.

14. When a game is completed, the result must be reported immediately to the director or a designated assistant. The manner in which the report is made (by signed scoresheet, entering result on pairing sheet, etc.) is at the director's discretion.

15. At the end of a playing session
   a. If, for any reason, it is impossible to determine how many moves have been made in a game that is to be continued or adjourned, it shall proceed from the final position on the board with the move number that begins the new time control.
   b. If unfinished games are to be adjourned and play resumed at a later time, FIDE Article 15 applies. Unless permitted by the director, a game must not be adjourned until the prescribed number of moves has been made by each player nor before the time specified for the end of the session.
   c. If unfinished games are to be continued, with or without a brief recess, and the

time between rounds is limited, games should be completed as quickly as possible. Provided prior announcement has been made, secondary time-control periods faster than the first time-control period may be used if they accord with the requirements of USCF Tournament Rule No. 7 above.
   d. Adjudications should be used only as a last resort.

16. If players agree on the result of an adjourned game before the time specified for its resumption, both players must notify the director (at a reasonable hour) or they may become liable to penalty under FIDE Article 17.2.

17. In all tournaments, every effort should be made to complete all unfinished games from previous rounds before the last round begins.

Chess Clocks

18. Before each round, all clocks should be placed at the right of the players with the black men and should be adjusted so that each unit will register six o'clock when the first time-control period expires. When the round begins, the clock of each player with the white men is started by his opponent if the latter is present or by an official if both players are absent. If White is present and Black is absent, White must immediately start his opponent's clock, but need not make his first move. When Black arrives, he stops his own clock and starts White's clock; White then makes his first move. Although White is not required to do so, he may, after starting Black's clock, make his first move before his opponent arrives (FIDE Article 14.3).

19. When a clock is not available at the beginning of the round, but is obtained or provided later, the following rules apply.
   a. If both players are present when the round begins, they start play immediately. If a clock becomes available later, the elapsed time is divided equally between the two players.
   b. If one player is absent when the round begins, he is charged with the elapsed time up to the moment of his arrival. The time from his arrival until a clock becomes available is divided equally between the two players.
   c. If both players are absent when the round begins, the player with the white men is charged with the elapsed time up to the moment of his arrival. If his opponent arrives still later, he is charged with the difference between White's arrival time

and his own. White makes his first move when Black arrives, and the time from then until a clock becomes available is divided equally between the two players.

20. *Alternate.* In a tournament with a large number of players, if the director believes that Rule No. 19 above cannot be applied, the following procedure may be substituted. However, written (and possibly verbal) announcement should be made in advance, and the same procedure must be used for all games.

 a. If both players are present when the round begins, but neither player has brought or obtained a clock, play starts immediately. When a clock becomes available, the director may require that the elapsed time be divided equally between the two players.

 b. If one player is absent when the round begins, play starts when the player who is present starts the clock he has brought or obtained. If he has not brought a clock and is unable to obtain one, play does not start until the opponent arrives. (No player may subtract time from a late opponent without starting a clock.) If a clock becomes available later, the director may require that the elapsed time be divided equally between the two players.

21. In any game without a clock at the beginning of the round, a player loses by default if he does not arrive within one hour after the time specified for the start of play. If neither player arrives within one hour, the game is lost by both (FIDE Article 17.2).

22. Players do not have the right to stop both clocks during a game except at adjournment (FIDE Article 15.1) or when claiming that a flag has fallen prematurely (Rule No. 23 below). Stopping both clocks at any other time may be done only by a director or referee in accordance with the rules or when he believes it is justifiable.

23. In the absence of an evident defect, the dropping of a clock's flag and the time on the clock indicate the moment at which the player's time-control period expires. A claim that a flag had fallen prematurely should be accepted only if there is a clear space between the minute hand and the left side of the hour marker when the flag drops. If there is no flag on a clock, the time-control period is deemed to have expired when there is a clear space between the right side of the hour marker and the minute hand.

Scorekeeping

24. Each player is required to record the moves of the game in the manner specified in FIDE Article 13.1 on the score sheet provided or approved by the tournament organizers. Either the algebraic system, recommended by FIDE, or the descriptive system of notation may be used.

25. A player in extreme time trouble is excused from writing down the moves, but should endeavor to make check marks on his score sheet to indicate the number of moves made. If, in the opinion of the referee, the player is not in extreme time trouble, the player must record the moves or he loses the game. (See FIDE Article 13.2 and USCF Tournament Rule No. 10a herein.)

 Except as provided in Supplement No. 4 of the FIDE Laws and in USCF Tournament Rule No. 26 below, no person may act as the deputy of a player in recording moves.

26. If a player's handicap prevents him from recording the moves, moving the men on the board, or operating his clock, the director may permit a deputy to perform such duties as the case may require. If the deputy records the moves, the opponent may have a deputy to keep score for him when in time trouble.

Time-Forfeits

27. Only his opponent (or a referee) should concern himself with the possibility that a player has lost a game on time. Spectators and *especially* participants in other games are not to speak or otherwise to interfere in possible time-forfeit situations.

28. When a player's time-control period expires and his opponent claims that he has not completed the required number of moves, play in the game should cease, and

 a. If a referee is present, he stops both clocks and decides whether or not the player has lost the game under the provisions of USCF Tournament Rule No. 29 below. If the referee decides not to forfeit, he starts the clock of the player having the move, and the game continues (or is adjourned) as if the next time-control period had commenced.

 b. If a referee is not present when the player's flag drops and the opponent wishes to claim a win on time, he must not record any moves on his score sheet and should immediately summon a referee to the board. When the latter arrives, he proceeds in the manner indicated in paragraph a above. If both flags are down when the referee arrives, a claim of a win on time should be considered only if the referee is satisfied that no moves were made after the second flag dropped.

29. When the flag of a player's clock drops at the expiration of his time-control period, he loses the game by a time-forfeit, and his opponent is declared the winner, provided that

   a. The opponent has a reasonably legible, accurate, and complete score of the game *when the flag falls.* (The director may permit a maximum of three incomplete move lines.)

   b. The opponent does not fill any moves missing from his score sheet after the flag is down, unless requested by the referee to record the omitted moves referred to in clause a above.

   c. The opponent's score sheet, after verification if necessary, proves that the player whose flag dropped had not completed the prescribed number of moves.

   If all the provisions stated herein are not fulfilled, no time-forfeit shall be given, and the game shall continue from the final position as if the next time control had commenced.

30. *Alternate (FIDE Procedure).* In a tournament in which referees can be present at all games where there is time trouble, the following procedure may be substituted. However, written (and possibly verbal) announcement should be made in advance.

   A referee will count the final moves of the game as they are played. When a player's flag drops, he will be forfeited if the referee's count shows that the player has not made the prescribed number of moves. An appeal from the referee's decision must be accompanied by a complete score of the game.

Drawn Games

31. A player who does not conform to the specifications of FIDE Article 17a.1 when proposing a draw by agreement (FIDE Article 12.2) is breaking the laws of chess and should be penalized or warned at the discretion of the director.

   An illegal proposal of a draw may, nevertheless, be accepted by the opponent. Thus,

   a. If a player proposes a draw while his opponent's clock is running, the opponent may agree to draw or reject the offer.

   b. If a player proposes a draw while his own clock is running, the opponent may accept or reject the offer, or he may postpone his decision until after the player has made a move.

In the above situations, the opponent may reject the illegal proposal orally or by making a move at his first opportunity. In the interval between the offer of a draw and the opponent's acceptance or rejection of it, the player who made the proposal cannot withdraw it.

32. It is unethical and unsportsmanlike to agree to a draw before a serious contest has begun. The same is also true of any agreement to "throw" a game. In cases of clear violations of the moral principles of the game, the director should impose penalties at his discretion.

Penalties

33. In a Swiss System tournament, any player who does not notify the director in advance that he will be unable to play in any round and then defaults the game by not appearing within one hour after the starting time (FIDE Article 17.2) may be fined the sum of five dollars ($5.00), payable to the sponsoring organization. The player will not be permitted to continue play in the tournament and may be barred by the sponsoring organization from any of its tournaments until the fine is paid.

34. Where penalties are not specifically defined by law or in these rules, the director has discretionary power to impose penalties such as the following for infractions of the FIDE Laws or USCF Tournament Rules and to maintain discipline:

   a. Cancel a game and rule that a new game be played in its stead.

   b. Declare a game lost by a player and won by his opponent.

   c. Declare a game lost by both players.

   d. Advance the time on a player's clock or give his opponent additional time.

   e. Expel a player from the tournament.

Appeals

35. A player may appeal for a review of any ruling made by the director or any of his assistants, provided that the appeal is made within thirty minutes after the conclusion of the session in which the ruling was made.

36. The director may appoint three persons acceptable to the appellant (and his opponent, if involved) to serve as an appeals committee. No committee member should participate in deciding an appeal if he is an interested party.

37. All appeals must be made through the director, and

   a. If the director believes an appeal is justified, he may reverse or modify any previous decision made by him or any of his assistants.

b. If the director does not believe an appeal is justified, but the player wishes to pursue the matter further, the director shall

  (1) Refer the appeal to the committee described in USCF Tournament Rule No. 36 above, in which case the committee may, if it finds the appeal groundless, authorize the director to penalize the player at his discretion;

  (2) Hold a hearing under his own jurisdiction, but only if he has not appointed an appeals committee.

38. When the appeals committee or the director hears an appeal, the facts should be determined first, and all persons, except members of the committee, the director, the appellant, his opponent, and the testifying witnesses, should be excluded from the hearing. When the appeals committee hears an appeal, it must accept as final the director's testimony as to anything said or done in his presence.

39. The appeals committee may hear and decide such part of an appeal as involves questions of fact or the exercise of the director's discretionary powers. It may not overrule the director on a point of law, but the committee may appeal his decision on a point of law to the USCF Tournament Direction Committee.

40. At a hearing conducted by the director, the director should hear and rule on—

a. Any part of a player's appeal dealing with a question of law.

b. An appeal based on a question of fact or the director's exercise of his discretionary power.

A player who has protested the director's decision on a point of law and whose protest has been disallowed may appeal to the USCF Tournament Direction Committee.

41. An appeal to the USCF Tournament Direction Committee may be made only on a point of law. The appeal must be made in writing and mailed to Committee Chairman Martin E. Morrison, US Chess Federation, 479 Broadway, Newburgh, New York 12550, within seven days. A copy of the appeal must be given to the tournament director, who shall forward to the Committee Chairman within fourteen days a written statement of the facts as found by the appeals committee or the director, as the case may be, together with an expression of the director's view on the legal aspects of the case. An appeal made in any other way shall not be acted upon.

Algebraic Notation

The horizontals (ranks) are numbered from 1 to 8, starting from the rank nearest White. The verticals (files) are lettered from a to h, starting at White's left (the QR file in algebraic is the a-file). The intersections of the horizontal and verticals give the individual squares their names, study the diagram.

Captures are indicated either by ":" or "x," and check is indicated by "+" instead of "ch." Pawn captures are given by naming only the two files involved. Study the sample game and use algebraic often—it's easier than you think.

Descriptive		Algebraic	
White	**Black**	**White**	**Black**
1 P-K4	P-K4	1 e4	e5
2 N-KB3	N-QB3	2 Nf3	Nc6
3 B-N5	P-QR3	3 Bb5	a6
4 BxN	QPxB	4 B:c6	dc
5 0-0	P-B3	5 0-0	f6
6 P-Q4	B-KN5	6 d4	Bg4
7 PxP	QxQ	7 de	Q:d1
8 RxQ	PxP	8 R:d1	fe
etc.		etc.	

Questions of interpretation of the official rules for playing chess and conducting tournaments and matches are frequently addressed to FIDE. In addition, the congress of the FIDE adopts amendments to the FIDE laws of chess from time to time which have the effect of streamlining the rules and clarifying their intent so that these contests can be run more fairly and efficiently. Some of the more important amendments are set forth here.

AMENDMENTS
TO THE FIDE LAWS OF CHESS
ADOPTED BY THE
1971 CONGRESS OF THE FIDE

1. In future, Article 8 should read:

The Touched Piece

Provided that he first warns his opponent, the player whose turn it is to move may adjust one or more pieces on their squares.

Except for the above case, if the player having the move touches one or more pieces, he must move or capture the first piece touched that can be moved or captured; and if he touches pieces of opposite colors, he must take the enemy piece with his own touched piece, or, if this is not possible, with another piece. If none of the touched pieces can be moved or captured, the player is free to make any legal move he chooses.

If a player wishes to claim a violation of this rule, he must do so before he touches a piece himself.

2. In the Rules of Play a new Article 20 has to be introduced. (The old Article 20 to be renumbered 21.)

The Touched Piece

The following rules are supplementary to those of Article 8:

1. Provided that he first warns his opponent, or the tournament controller if the opponent is absent, the player whose turn it is to move may adjust one or more pieces on their squares.

Except for the above case, if the player whose turn it is to move touches

a) one or more of his own pieces, he must move the first that can be moved; but if the first two touched pieces are the King and a Rook, the player must castle with that Rook, or, if this is illegal, move the King.

b) one or more of his opponent's pieces, he must capture the first that can be taken.

c) one of his own pieces and one of his opponent's pieces, he must capture the latter with the former, or, if this is illegal, with another piece; and if it is impossible to capture the enemy piece, the player must move his own touched piece.

d) one or more pieces of one color and two or more pieces of the opposite color, the player's opponent shall specify

1) the touched piece that must be moved or captured; or

2) the capture that must be made by two touched pieces.

In the situations of clauses a) and b) above, if it cannot be determined which moveable or captureable piece was touched first, the opponent shall specify which touched piece must be moved or captured, as the case may be. This provision does not apply to the castling move referred to in clause a).

2. In all the situations of section no. 1 above:

a) If the player touches a piece of his own with no legal moves, or any enemy piece that cannot be captured, the situation shall be regarded as one in which the player did not touch the said piece.

b) If none of the player's touched pieces can be legally moved and none of the touched enemy pieces can be captured, the player is free to make any move he chooses.

3. The enforcement of the foregoing regulations by the tournament controller does not require a claim to be made, but if a player wishes to claim a violation, he must do so before he touches a piece himself.

When a player is accused by his opponent, or by an official, of breaking any of these regulations, the tournament controller shall stop the clocks of both players until he has decided what action shall be taken; and if the tournament controller rules that the opponent must specify the move or capture to be made, the latter's clock shall be started and remain running until he announces his selection and starts the other player's clock.

3. The Commission accepted an improved English translation of the Rules for playing chess between sighted and blind players (Supplement 4), which was presented by the British Chess Federation.

Supplement No. 4
Rules for Playing Chess between Sighted and Blind Players

In competitive chess between sighted and blind players the use of two chessboards shall be obligatory, the sighted player using a normal chessboard, while the blind player uses one with securing apertures.

The following regulations shall govern play:—

(1) The moves shall be announced clearly, repeated by the opponent, and executed on his board.

(2) On the blind player's board a piece shall be deemed "touched" when it has been taken out of the securing aperture.

(3) A move shall be deemed executed when:—
    (a) a piece is placed into a securing aperture;
    (b) in the case of a capture, the captured piece has been removed from the board of the player who has the move;
    (c) the move has been announced.

Only after this shall the opponent's clock be started.

(4) A chess clock with flag, made specially for the blind, shall be admissible.

(5) The blind player may keep the score of the game in braille or on a tape recorder.

(6) A slip of the tongue in announcing a move must be corrected immediately and before starting the clock of the opponent.

(7) If, during a game, different positions should arise on the two boards, such differences have to be corrected with the assistance of the controller and by consulting both players' game scores. In resolving such differences, the player who has written down the correct move, but executed the wrong one, has to accept certain disadvantages.

(8) If, when such discrepancies occur, the two game scores are also found to differ, the moves shall be retraced up to the point where the two scores agree, and the controller shall readjust the clocks accordingly.

(9) The blind player shall have the right to make use of an assistant who shall have the following duties:
    (a) to make the moves of the blind player on the board of the opponent;
    (b) to announce the moves of the sighted player;
    (c) to keep the score for the blind player and start his opponent's clock;
    (d) to inform the blind player, at his request, of the number of moves made and the time used up by both players;
    (e) to claim the game in cases where the time limit has been exceeded;
    (f) to carry out the necessary formalities in cases where the game is adjourned.

(10) If the blind player does not require any assistance, the sighted player may make use of an assistant who shall announce his moves and make the blind player's moves on the board.

INTERPRETATIONS
OF THE FIDE LAWS OF CHESS
Made By the Permanent Commission of the FIDE
For the Laws of the Game
ADOPTED BY THE

1970 CONGRESS OF THE FIDE

1. *Question.* The British Chess Federation hereby asks the Permanent Commission for the Rules of Chess for a ruling on a question relating to Article 16.5 of the Rules of Chess. It concerns the question as to what measures should be taken when the conditions indicated in the said clause are only partially fulfilled, in that the envelope containing the sealed move has disappeared, but it is still possible to establish by an agreement between the players the position at the adjournment and the times used until that moment.

Answer. The Commission decided that the game under such circumstances has to be continued.

2. *Question.* What are the consequences when a player or team withdraws or is expelled from a tournament?

Answer. This question was answered *preliminarily* in the minutes of FIDE Congress 1969. Now the Commission declares that this decision is *final.*

["a. If a player has *not* completed at least 50% of his games when he leaves the tournament, his score remains in the tournament table, but the points scored by him or against him are not counted in the final standings.* For the games not played or finished the player, as well as his opponent, gets a /–/ in the tournament table.

["b. If a player *has* completed at least 50% of his games when he leaves the tournament, his score remains in the tournament table and will be counted in the final standings. For the games not played the opponents will get a /1/, and the player himself will get a /0/.

["c. The same rules apply equally when a team is concerned instead of a player."]

3. *Question.* The Yugoslavian Chess Federation asked the following question: "A player, referring to the Rules of Chess, has asked his opponent to make first his move and only then write it down on his score sheet. It is thought not to be correct first to write down the move and only then make it on the board. The referee of the tournament in question judged the case to be insignificant. In order to be exact, it is desirable, however, that the Rules Commission give its interpretation."

Answer. The Commission is of the opinion that the players should have the right of choice (that every player who has the move has the choice—1971 formulation).

*However, all played games should be reported for rating purposes.—MEM

1. At the request of Prof. Euwe the Commission discussed the following case:

In a game between player A (white) and player B (black), B played on the 45th move . . . c2-cl. However, he neglected to immediately exchange the pawn for a Queen. On his score sheet he had written 45 . . . c2-clQ and punched his clock afterwards. Then he left the board. At the time, his opponent was not present. When player A returned to the board, he protested because B had not immediately exchanged the pawn on cl, though B told him the piece on cl was a Queen. The tournament controller decided as follows: Player A's clock was restored to the position it had before the move . . . c2-cl was made. Player B had to make his move 45 . . . c2-clQ again, as it was obvious that he intended to promote that pawn to a Queen. Then the game was resumed in the normal way.

The Commission confirmed the decision of the tournament controller.

2. With regard to the case mentioned under 1, the Commission gives the following interpretation as to Article 6c of the Rules of Play:

In a competition, if a new piece is not immediately available, the player should ask for the assistance of the tournament controller before making his move. If this request is made and there is any appreciable delay in obtaining the new piece, the tournament controller should stop both clocks until the required piece is given to the player having the move. If no request is made and the player makes his move and punches his clock without exchanging the promoted pawn for a new piece, he is breaking the laws of chess and should be given a warning or a disciplinary penalty, such as the advancement of the time on his clock. In any case, the opponent's clock should be set back to the time it registered immediately before the player punched his clock, the position on the board should be re-established to what it was before the player moved his pawn, and the clock of the player having the move should be started. The player should then make his move correctly, in the manner specified in Article 6c.

3. With regard to a proposal of the Cuban Chess Federation concerning Article 11.2 of the Rules of Play, the Commission states:

If a player shakes hands with his opponent, this is not to be considered as equal to resigning the game as meant in Article 11.2.

4. With regard to a question from the Panama Chess Federation concerning Article 6 of the Rules of Play, the Commission answers as follows:

If a player in castling starts with touching the Rook, he shall receive a warning from the tournament controller, but the castling shall be considered to be valid.

If a player intending to castle touches King and Rook at the same time and it then appears the castling is illegal, the player has to move his King. If the King has no legal move, the fault has no consequences.

5. The Commission decided to give an interpretation of Article 14 under 5) and 6):

With regard to Article 14.5 and 6, the tournament controller shall endeavor to check all clocks periodically to make sure that they are operating properly.

A clock with an obvious defect shall be replaced and the time used by each player up to the moment when the game was interrupted shall be indicated on the new clock as accurately as possible.

If one unit of the defective clock has stopped, the corresponding unit of the new clock shall be advanced so that the total time indicated by the two units is equal to the time the session of the competition had been in progress.

If both units have stopped, the difference between the total of the times registered by the defective clock and the elapsed time of the session shall be divided in half and each unit of the new clock advanced by this amount.

If any of the above clock adjustments would result in a player exceeding the time limit or if the time used by each player cannot be accurately determined, the tournament controller may set the hands of the new clock in accordance with his best judgment.

6. At the request of the Cuban Chess Federation, the Commission gives the following interpretation to Article 17a.2 and Article 14.4 of the Rules of Play.

A player who is due to make his last move before the time control and who claims a draw in the manner prescribed in a) and b) of Article 12.3 must make his last move on the chessboard, without stopping his clock.

If the tournament controller believes the player had sufficient time to stop his clock before the flag falls, he may rule that the player had completed his move, the provisions of Article 14.4 not being applicable in this situation. The tournament controller should then investigate the claim of a draw, and if the claim is found to be incorrect, the game shall be continued or adjourned, even if the claimant's flag has fallen.

7. At the request of the Chess Federation of the USSR, the Commission recommends all affiliated federations to promote the use of the algebraic chess notation as much as possible. In particular, young chess players should be encouraged to use the algebraic notation.

ADOPTED BY THE
1972 CONGRESS OF THE FIDE

1. *Question.* Concerning Article 13.2 of the rules about keeping the score: Is a player in time-trouble obliged to punch his clock with the same hand with which he keeps score?
Answer. The Laws of Chess make no such requirement, whether or not the player is in time-trouble. Nor is there any law that requires a player to punch his clock with the hand he uses to make moves on the board.

2. *Question.* With regard to Article 14.6, is the sudden illness during the course of a game or the sudden decease of a close relative covered by this Article?
Answer. With regard to Article 14.6: If the sudden illness during the course of a game is deemed to be of short duration, then the answer is YES. But if it is not regarded as likely to be brief, the answer is NO. In this case and—also in the case of the sudden decease of a close relative—the matter must be left to the discretion of the arbiter.

3. *Question.* In a recent game, the player with the white pieces claimed that his opponent violated Article 20.1a by touching a piece, then moving a different piece. Black denied the accusation, and a Director was called to the board. There was no independent witness of any kind to the alleged violation, so the Director rejected the claim for lack of evidence.

White then claimed that the situation is covered by the last paragraph of Article 20.1 in which it is stated that ". . . if it cannot be determined which piece which could be moved or captured was touched first, the opponent should specify which touched piece must be moved or captured, as the case may be." The Director summarily rejected this claim.
Answer. The Director was correct in both instances. As in the case of all other laws, unbiased evidence is required to support any claim by a player that his opponent broke the law. If the accused player denies the allegation, and it is impossible to prove otherwise by the testimony of an official or other disinterested witness, it is just a question of one player's word against that of his opponent. An unsubstantiated claim would have to be rejected.

The second claim is frivolous. The quoted words from the last paragraph of Article 20.2 refer only to a situation in which there is evidence to support a claim that two or more men were touched, but it is impossible to determine which was touched first.

GLOSSARY

INDEX

Bold faced numbers indicate related diagrams.

A

SUGGESTED READING

CHESS OPENINGS: THEORY AND PRACTICE, I. A. Horowitz,
    Simon & Schuster, New York, 1964.

THE IDEAS BEHIND THE CHESS OPENINGS, Reuben Fine,
    David McKay, Philadelphia, 1943.

CHESS FUNDAMENTALS, José Raul Capablanca, Harcourt,
    New York, 1959.

MY SYSTEM, Aron Nimzowitsch, David McKay, New York, 1947.

CHESS PRAXIS, Aron Nimzowitsch, Printing Craft, Ltd., London,
    1936.

MARSHALL'S BEST GAMES OF CHESS, Frank Marshall, Dover
    Publications, Inc., New York, 1942.

THE ART OF SACRIFICE, Rudolf Spielmann, Bell, London,
    1935.

COMMON SENSE IN CHESS, Emanuel Lasker, David McKay,
    Philadelphia, 1946.

THE ROAD TO CHESS MASTERY, Max Euwe and Walter
    Meiden, David McKay, New York, 1966.